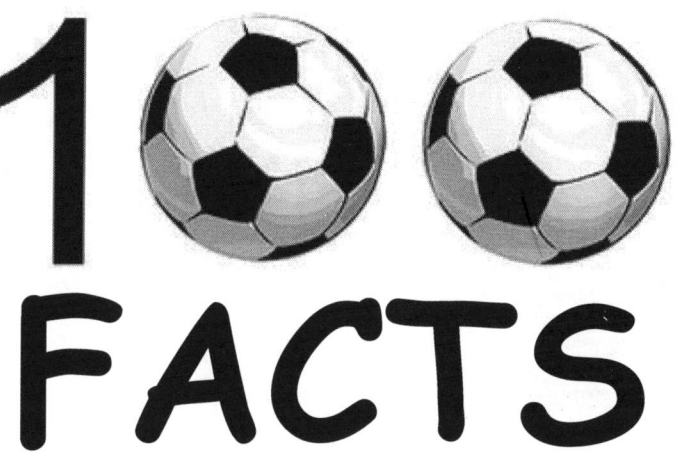

FACTS

HEARTS

100 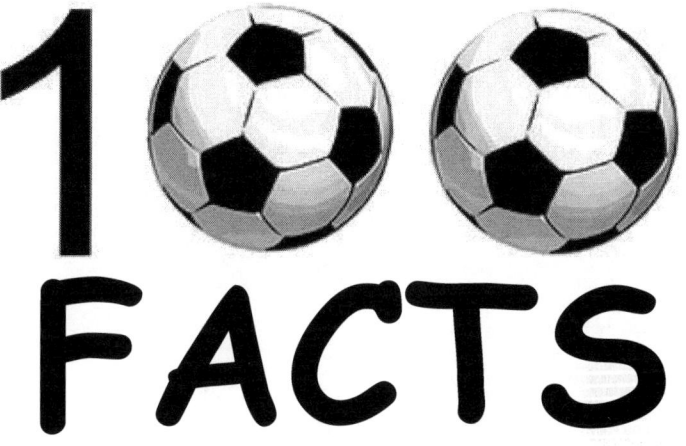 FACTS

HEARTS

Steve Horton

Bedford, England

First published in Great Britain in 2020
by Wymer Publishing
www.wymerpublishing.co.uk
Wymer Publishing is a trading name of Wymer (UK) Ltd

First edition. Copyright © 2020 Steve Horton / Wymer Publishing.

ISBN 978-1-912782-48-2

Edited by Jerry Bloom.

The Author hereby asserts his rights to be identified
as the author of this work in accordance with sections
77 to 78 of the Copyright, Designs & Patents Act 1988.

All rights reserved. No part of this publication may be
reproduced or transmitted in any form or by any means,
electronic or mechanical, including photocopying, or any
information storage and retrieval system, without written
permission from the publisher.

This publication is sold subject to the condition that it shall not,
by way of trade or otherwise, be lent, re-sold, hired out or
otherwise circulated without the publishers prior consent in any
form of binding or cover other than that in which it is published
and without a similar condition including this condition
being imposed on the subsequent purchaser.

Typeset and Design by Andy Bishop / 1016 Sarpsborg
Printed and bound by CMP, Poole, Dorset

A catalogue record for this book is available from the British Library.

Sketches by Becky Welton. © 2014.

FACT 1

1874
HEART
OF MIDLOTHIAN

Heart of Midlothian, to give Hearts their full title, were formed in 1874 and is the oldest association football club in Edinburgh.

In December 1873 the first football match in Edinburgh played under association rules took place at Bonnington. It was an exhibition game between Queens Park and Clydesdale and amongst the crowd of 200 were members of the Heart of Midlothian Quadrille Assembly Club, a dance group.

Some of those members already played a form of football but decided to start a club playing the association code. The name Heart of Midlothian comes from a mosaic on the Royal Mile, marking the historic entrance to the Old Tollbooth Gaol. The club are generally referred to as Hearts as well as their nicknames of 'Jam Tarts' and 'Jambos.'

Captained by Tom Purdie, Hearts began playing fixtures at East Meadows, part of The Meadows public park south of the city centre. The club headquarters was Anderson's Coffee House and Tavern, at the corner of St Patrick Street and West Crosscauseway.

The following year, 1875, club secretary Hugh Wylie successfully applied to join the Edinburgh and Scottish Football Associations, allowing them to take part in structured competitions.

FACT 2

1875
THE FIRST EDINBURGH DERBY

The first game between Hearts and their Edinburgh rivals Hibernian, more commonly known as Hibs, was at East Meadows on Christmas Day 1875.

Hibs were formed in August 1875 by members of the Catholic Young Men's Society. However due to their Irish heritage, they were denied entry to both the Scottish and Edinburgh Football Associations, who even ordered their members not to play against the new club.

Hearts broke ranks and agreed to a friendly with Hibs at East Meadows, on Christmas Day. Despite Hearts having only eight players available the game still kicked off as scheduled. Numerical disadvantage didn't affect Hearts, who held on for twenty minutes when the other three players arrived. They went on to win the game 1-0.

Throughout 1876 Hibs officials canvassed other clubs in the Edinburgh area and gained sympathy amongst those who felt nobody in the community should be excluded from football. This led to their eventual acceptance by the Edinburgh FA and subsequently Scottish FA in 1877.

The Edinburgh Derby is now one of the longest running rivalries in world football. Games are now played in packed modern stadiums before crowds of up to 20,000. At Whalebone Arch in The Meadows, a plaque commemorates the first meeting of the two clubs that was played in much different surroundings.

FACT 3
1878 EDINBURGH CUP WINNERS

Hearts won their first trophy in 1878, eventually beating Hibs in the fourth replay of a marathon Edinburgh Cup final.

The first game at Mayfield Park on 9th February ended in a 0-0 draw. A week later the sides met again at the same venue, where 1,000 spectators witnessed a 1-1 draw. Hearts declined to play extra time, opting instead to replay again the following Saturday.

On 23rd February the teams were back at Mayfield Park and this time the crowd increased to 1,200. Hibs led 1-0 at half time but Hearts equalised late in the second half, triggering a pitch invasion. After order was eventually restored, there was no further scoring meaning a third replay was necessary.

The next time the teams tried to settle things was on 6th April at Merchiston. Again it was a 1-1 draw, watched by 1,500 fans. Two weeks later at Powburn, where heavy rain reduced the crowd to 1,200, Hearts twice came from behind to win 3-2 and claim the trophy. The scorer of the all-important winning goal was George Mitchell.

The following year Hibs got their revenge, beating Hearts in the final after a replay. The competition is now known as the Edinburgh Shield and contested by the youth sides of the two clubs.

FACT 4

1880 RECORD VICTORY

Hearts record victory was in an Edinburgh Cup tie on 30th October 1880, when they beat Anchor by the astonishing score line of 21-0.

The second round tie took place at Old Powderhall but received very little press coverage. The extent of the report in The Scotsman was that "the tie resulted in an easy victory for the Hearts by twenty-one goals to nothing." Research by historians has been unable to establish any of the scorers or the team line up.

In the following round Hearts were knocked out of the competition by Hibs, who won 3-1 at Old Powderhall in front of 7,000 spectators.

Two seasons later Hearts hit twenty in the Edinburgh Cup again, thrashing Holyrood 20-2. Other huge victories in the 1880s included an 18-0 win against Vale of Midlothian in the Edinburgh Shield and a 14-0 Scottish Cup victory over Addiewell.

In league competition Hearts have never been able to even match halve the 21-goal tally. The closest they have come is ten goals on four occasions, most recently a 10-0 win over Cowdenbeath at Tynecastle in 2014-15.

FACT 5

1881
NEW YEAR IN ENGLAND

Hearts ventured south of the border for the first time in 1881, when they played two games in England in January.

As revellers in Edinburgh took advantage of the mild weather to enjoy their Hogmanay celebrations, Hearts travelled to Birmingham. Their opponents in a friendly on the first day of 1881 at Perry Barr were Aston Villa, one of the best teams in the English Midlands.

In the first half Hearts were overwhelmed and trailed 4-1 at the break. However in the second period the game was more even and their performance was described by the Daily Review as creditable. It finished 4-2, with John Alexander scoring five minutes from the end. Afterwards both sets of players were entertained by the owner of the Witton Ammunition Works.

Two days later Hearts were in Lancashire to take on Blackburn Rovers at Alexandra Meadows. Syndicated reports in English newspapers said that Jake Reid had a good game in goal while Will Ronaldson, Andrew Lees and Alex McNeil were strong in attack. Their efforts were in vain though as Hearts lost the game 2-1, Ronaldson scoring their goal.

FACT 6

1881
OLD
TYNECASTLE

In 1881 Hearts moved to the Gorgie area of Edinburgh and started playing their home games at a ground that is now usually referred to as 'Old Tynecastle.'

Tynecastle Park, to give it the full title, was not a purpose-built venue and had been used by various teams, including St Bernard's, to stage fixtures. However by taking ownership the Hearts now had somewhere to call home.

The first games at their new home, which was situated where Wardlaw Street now stands, took place on 9th April. A reserve eleven beat Lancefield 6-2 followed by the fist team beating Hanover 8-0. Hearts played three more fixtures at Old Tynecastle in 1881, winning them all.

Due to Tynecastle being away from the densely populated areas, Hearts sometimes played double fixtures at the venue and reduced prices to attract more fans. For the opening fixtures, men were charged sixpence and ladies admitted for free. During the summer, Hearts staged an athletic meeting to raise extra funds. Events included flat races, hop step and jump, and a sack race.

They remained there until 1886, when they moved to the other side of Gorgie Road and a new site leased from Edinburgh Corporation, who built tenements on the old one.

FACT 7
1882 RECORD DEFEAT

Hearts record defeat was on 21st October 1882, when they were thrashed 8-1 by Vale of Leven in the Scottish Cup third round.

Hearts had knocked out St Bernard's and Addiewell to reach the third round, thrashing the latter 14-0. However they knew this trip to West Dunbartonshire to face Vale of Leven, winners of the Scottish Cup three times in the 1870s, would be much more of a contest.

The match was played in a torrential downpour that limited the crowd to just 200 hardy souls. Hearts were undone by their opponents' superior passing and were 1-0 down after just three minutes. They trailed 3-1 at half time and conceded five more without reply in the second period.

Despite the crushing margin, the *Daily Review* was complimentary of the performance of the Hearts players. It described how "they played pluckily till the very last" and "although too slow in tackling, did their best to intercept the Vale forwards."

Although Hearts have lost by bigger score lines in wartime competition and friendlies, this crushing loss is generally regarded as the club's record defeat.

FACT 8

1884
SUSPENDED FOR PROFESSIONALISM

Hearts were suspended by the Scottish FA in 1884 for making payments to players, which was against the rules at the time.

Football in Scotland was strictly amateur and many of the best players were moving to England. Although the game was amateur there, clubs were getting around the rules by arranging jobs for players in factories but in reality they did very little work.

Hibs were dominating the Edinburgh football scene and Hearts, like many others, had to begin making payments to players to retain the best ones.

After Hearts beat Dunfermline 11-1 away from home in a Scottish Cup tie in October 1884, the Fife club made a complaint to the SFA. The Hearts committee admitted paying Chris McNee and James Maxwell 26 shillings per week. They club were disqualified from the competition and suspended from the SFA for two years.

Following the election of a new committee, Hearts were readmitted to the SFA. They were allowed into the Scottish Cup for the following season but were beaten in the first round by Hibs. The SFA finally bowed to pressure and allowed players to be professional in 1893, eight years after England had done so.

FACT 9
1886
TYNECASTLE PARK

Hearts moved to the venue they continue to call home in 1886, their first fixture being a friendly with English side Bolton Wanderers.

As the city's population grew westwards, the site of Old Tynecastle was required by Edinburgh Corporation to build tenements. However Hearts were compensated by being able to lease land on the other side of Gorgie Road where they could develop their own purpose built ground.

The new venue was opened on 10th April with a friendly against Bolton, who were touring Scotland. An advert in the *Edinburgh Evening News* said that kick off was at 4 o'clock prompt and that admission was sixpence. Anyone wishing to transfer to the grandstand would have to pay another sixpence.

The *Manchester Courier & Lancashire General Advertiser* described the new venue as 'splendid.' Bolton were confident of success, having beaten Rangers the previous day, however Hearts raced into a 3-0 half time lead. Bolton pulled one back in the second half but Hearts restored their three goal advantage and the game finished 4-1.

Tynecastle Park remains Hearts home to the present day and has a capacity of just under 20,000. It was officially renamed Tynecastle Stadium in the mid 1990s, but this was never popular and reverted back to Tynecastle Park in 2017. Generally though, it is referred to as just 'Tynecastle.'

FACT 10
1886
THE ENGLISH FA CUP

Hearts tried their luck south of the border in 1886-87 when they competed in the English FA Cup for the first time, but they were well beaten in their first-round tie.

Scottish cubs had been allowed to enter the English FA Cup since it began in 1871-72, but prior to 1885 only Queens Park had ever entered. Their success in reaching successive finals led to other Scottish clubs trying their luck.

Hearts entered the 1885-86 competition and were drawn to play away at Padiham but withdrew under pressure from the Scottish FA. In 1886-87 however, they opted to go ahead with their tie at Darwen, semi-finalists a few years earlier.

The game took place at Darwen's Barley Bank ground on 30th October 1886 and Hearts took the lead after ten minutes. However the home side hit back and by half time Hearts were 4-1 down.

In the second half Hearts were unlucky to have two goals disallowed and at the other end Darwen were clinical, scoring another three goals. The 7-1 score line flattered the opposition and the *Edinburgh Evening News* suggested that some "sifting and organisation" was needed of the Hearts team.

This would be the only time Hearts entered the English FA Cup as the following season the Scottish FA barred any of their members from taking part.

FACT 11
1887
THE FIRST INTERNATIONAL

The first Hearts player to represent Scotland was Tom Jenkinson, who was selected to play against Ireland at Hampden Park on 19th February 1887.

Jenkinson made his Hearts debut as a teenager in 1884 and played at outside right. His attention was drawn to the national side selectors when he scored a hat-trick in a Scottish Cup tie against Edina in November 1886.

Despite fine weather, the British Championship match with Ireland attracted a crowd of just 1,000. Jenkinson made an immediate impression, crossing for William Watt to score the opening goal within the first five minutes.

Jenkinson thought he had put Scotland further ahead but his effort was disallowed for offside. Ireland then equalised, but just before half time he did restore Scotland's lead with a tremendous shot that went in off the post. In the second half he almost scored again but his shot bounced off the crossbar and over. Scotland eventually ran out 4-1 winners.

This game turned out to be Jenkinson's only appearance for Scotland. He left Hearts in 1891 and spent some time in England before emigrating to Australia.

FACT 12
1890
THE SCOTTISH LEAGUE

In 1890 Hearts were founder members of the Scottish Football League and finished sixth in their first season.

The English Football League was founded in 1888 and there were fears the best Scottish players may move south of the border. The secretary of Renton invited thirteen clubs, including Hearts, to a meeting about forming a league in Scotland. Of those thirteen, Clyde and Queens Park declined the invitation.

In April 1890 the Scottish Football League was formed and there would be eleven clubs for the inaugural season. Hearts were the only club from the east of Scotland to be involved. Another Edinburgh side, St Bernard's, failed to gain election.

Hearts lost their first three games in the new league competition; 5-2 against Rangers at Ibrox, 5-0 against Celtic at Tynecastle then 3-1 at Dumbarton. They recovered however to win home games against Cowlairs (4-0) and Vale of Leven (8-1).

Hearts eventually finished the season in sixth place out of ten teams. Renton, who started the season, were expelled after five games for playing against St Bernard's against the wishes of the Scottish FA and other league members.

FACT 13
1891 SCOTTISH CUP WINNERS

In 1891 Hearts won the Scottish Cup for the first time, beating favourites Dumbarton in the final at the Second Hampden Park.

Hearts had a straightforward route to the final and didn't face Scottish League opposition until the last four, when they beat Third Lanark 4-1. They were clearly the underdogs for the final, which was against unbeaten league leaders Dumbarton on 7th February.

In the first half, Hearts took the game to their opponents and the play of the forwards was faultless. Neutrals in the crowd marvelled at Hearts passing game, as opposed to the dribbling that they were more accustomed to. Willie Mason scored after fifteen minutes and at half time Dumbarton were fortunate to be just one goal behind.

The second half was a different story, with Dumbarton dominating the midfield only to see their forwards wasteful with chances. Hearts struggled to create any meaningful attacks, but they held on for victory. Supporters took to the pitch and carried the players off shoulder high.

Two hours after the game ended, the team was presented with the cup at a Glasgow hotel before boarding a chartered train. They arrived back in Edinburgh at 10.30pm, where thousands of fans had congregated outside Princes Street station.

FACT 14
1892
THE FIRST SENDING OFF

On 23rd April 1892 George Goodfellow was anything but what his name suggested when he became the first Hearts player to be sent off in a league match.

The game against Rangers had been played in a good-natured way and in its closing stages when Goodfellow, a full back, got sent off. News reports state that it was an unfortunate incident in which he "made a rush towards McCreadie and kicked him."

When Goodfellow was ordered off the field by the referee Mr McLean there was no adverse reaction from the crowd. It was more a reaction of surprise as he was said to usually play a gentlemanly game. There was no further scoring and both teams had to finish the game with ten men as McCreadie was unable to continue.

Although Goodfellow was the first Hearts player to be sent off in a league game, one of his teammates had been ordered to leave the field earlier in the season. In December 1891 Davie Russell had been sent off for fighting in an East of Scotland Shield game against Mossend Swifts.

FACT 15
1895 LEAGUE CHAMPIONS

Hearts won the Scottish League Championship for the first time in 1894-95, leading the table for the whole of the campaign.

Hearts had a magnificent start to the season, winning their first eleven games. This magnificent run finally ended with a 4-2 home defeat to Clyde.

On 16th February Hearts beat Celtic 4-0 at Tynecastle to put them on the brink of securing a first championship. They were even on course for a league and cup double, but then lost the Scottish Cup semi-final to St Bernard's.

Hearts had the perfect opportunity to get over the semi-final defeat on 23rd March, when just a point against Clyde at Barrowfield would be enough to secure the title. They trailed 1-0 at half time after a tough battle against the wind. Despite having it on their side in the second half, Hearts conceded two more to trail 3-0 after an hour. They fought back but could only narrow the deficit to 3-2 by full time.

The disappointment of defeat was soon forgotten when news was received that Celtic could only draw 1-1 with Rangers, meaning Hearts could not be caught at the top of the table. They eventually finished the season with fifteen wins from eighteen games, five points clear of Celtic.

FACT 16
1896 SCOTTISH CUP WINNERS IN EDINBURGH

In 1896 Hearts won the Scottish Cup for the second time. They beat city rivals Hibs in the only final of the competition that has ever taken place outside Glasgow.

The venue for the final was Logie Green, home of St Bernard's FC. It attracted a crowd of 16,034, with *The Scotsman* reporting that "they met in every way the requirements of the Association, and that, as a matter of fact, everybody who applied gained admission."

Hearts took the lead after just three minutes, Davie Baird converting a penalty that was awarded for handball. They continued to dominate play in the first half but the score remained 1-0 at the interval.

Hibs started the second half well and Hearts had to withstand a lot of pressure. However after 63 minutes Hearts broke away and Alex King scored with a shot that was too strong for the keeper to hold. Hibs were deflated after this and Willie Michael headed a third just two minutes afterwards.

The noise that greeted Michael's goal was deafening, reports stating that "Hats, sticks, and handkerchiefs were thrown wildly in the air" by the Hearts supporters. Hibs scored a late consolation to draw one of the best finals to date to a close.

FACT 17
1896
BOBBY WALKER

One of Hearts greatest ever players, Bobby Walker, made his debut as a seventeen-year-old on 3rd October 1896.

Walker was still three months short of his eighteenth birthday when he was selected to play against St Bernard's at Tynecastle. He scored one and had another disallowed as Hearts won 5-2.

Hearts were champions in 1896-97 but Walker was limited to just three appearances. However as he grew in experience and ability, he was indispensable for the next sixteen seasons. Although slightly built, he was comfortable on the ball and could weave in and out of defenders with ease, wrong foot whole defences in one movement and deliver a precision pass.

Walker was the first Hearts player to score 100 league goals and his total of 33 against Hibs remains a record if local competitions are included. One of his finest hours for Hearts was the Scottish Cup final of 1901, when they beat Celtic 4-3.

Walker was capped 29 times by Scotland, more than any other Hearts player until Steven Pressley in 2006. A one club man, he played 328 league games for Hearts, scoring 124 goals. After retiring from playing he became director of the club in 1920.

FACT 18
1897 CHAMPIONS AGAIN

Hearts won their second Scottish League Championship in 1896-97. Unlike in 1895, it was a much closer title race with three teams involved when the season reached its climax.

In the first half of the season Hearts away form let them down and they were beaten at Celtic, Rangers and Hibs, who all fancied their chances of winning the title. They then won eight games out of nine to set up a thrilling finish. There was even the possibility of a three-way tie between Hearts, Hibs and Celtic.

Going into their last game of the season against Clyde at Tynecastle, Hearts were level on 26 points with Hibs, who had completed their fixtures. Celtic had 24 points but with two games to play. If all three teams finished with the same points, then a mini tournament would be required to determine who would be champions.

On 20th February Hearts comfortably beat Clyde 5-0, meaning Hibs were out of the running. They then received the surprising news that Celtic had lost 1-0 at home to Dundee and that they were champions for the second time in three seasons.

FACT 19
1898
SCOTLAND'S FIRST BLACK PROFESSIONAL PLAYER

In March 1898 Hearts signed winger John Walker, the first black professional footballer in Scotland.

Walker was signed from Leith Athletic of the Second Division, with reports of the fee paid ranging from £50 to £80. His debut was on 29th October, when he scored in a 5-1 win over Hibs at Easter Road. The *Edinburgh Evening News* described his play as "fast, nimble and accurate."

Although there had been other black players who had played in Scotland before him, they had been either before professionalism, or for Queens Park who were strictly amateur.

The goal against Hibs was his only one in six league appearances at outside left that 1898-99 season, when Hearts finished second to Rangers. The limited appearances were down to a tendency for individual flair rather than team passing. As such, directors preferred to use David Baird or John Blair in his position.

In the summer of 1899 Walker signed for Lincoln City in the English Second Division, but he failed to settle there. He returned to Scotland and died of tuberculosis in August 1900, when he was just 22 years old.

FACT 20
1901 SCOTTISH CUP WINNERS

Hearts won the Scottish Cup for the third time in 1900-01 when they beat Celtic in a seven-goal thriller, Mark Bell netting the winner a minute from time.

5,000 Hearts fans travelled on special trains for the final that took place at Ibrox. They also had the support of many neutrals in the crowd that was limited to 16,000 due to bad weather. Celtic fans were also unhappy at the one shilling admission charge.

Bobby Walker opened the scoring for Hearts after twelve minutes. Celtic equalised through Willie McOustra but seven minutes before half time Bell's fierce shot was saved by the keeper only to bounce off a defender back into the net.

Early in the second half Charlie Thompson scored a third for Hearts. However Celtic fought back, Jimmy Quinn scoring with nineteen minutes to go then Sandy McMahon heading an equaliser with nine minutes remaining.

A replay looked inevitable but with a minute to go Walker's shot could only be parried by the keeper and Bell was on hand to score the rebound. It was no more than Hearts deserved, with Walker having made an outstanding performance. Later that evening the victorious team arrived at Waverley Station where they were greeted by a band and 10,000 fans who braved the rainfall.

FACT 21
1902 FOOTBALL WORLD CHAMPIONSHIP

In 1902 Hearts were declared as the best football team in world when they beat English FA Cup winners Tottenham Hotspur.

This was the second time Hearts had taken part in what was billed as the Football World Championship, even though only teams from England and Scotland competed. In 1895 they were invited as league champions but were beaten 5-3 by Sunderland at Tynecastle.

For the first time the event was a two-legged affair. On 2nd September 1901 the sides drew 0-0 at White Hart Lane, but the return game at Tynecastle didn't take place until 2nd January 1902. Hearts had played Hibs the day before and made a number of changes to the side, but the game still attracted a good crowd of 8,000.

Hearts grew in strength as the game went on and deservedly took the lead towards the end of the first half through Charlie Thomson. Soon after the break Bobby Walker scored with a tremendous shot and Tom Lorn quickly added a third. Tottenham, who were understandably tired given they had been 200 miles away at Everton the previous day, scored late on from a penalty.

The *Edinburgh Evening News* reported that Tottenham's forwards had been "very tightly held" by the Hearts defenders and that although an exhibition match, it was "a very good draw from a financial point of view."

FACT 22
1903
HAIL HELPS OUT IN THE FINAL

After winning their first three Scottish Cup finals, Hearts finally had to settle for being runners up in 1903. However they made Rangers work hard for their success, taking advantage of a hail induced stoppage in the first game of a final that required two replays.

At Celtic Park on 11th April, Hearts were fortunate to still be level at half time as Rangers were dominating the game. A minute into the second half Rangers took the lead and looked set for victory. However, the game was then held up for five minutes due to a hailstorm.

Whilst the players sought shelter in the pavilion, Hearts made some positional changes and came out stronger. It paid dividends and Bobby Walker equalised with eight minutes remaining. There was no extra time and Hearts were delighted both with the draw and the prospect of sharing more gate receipts.

The following week the sides met again at Celtic Park, drawing 0-0 in a game of few chances. Again there was no extra time and the *Edinburgh Evening News* was critical of Hearts for not demanding the second replay should take place in Edinburgh.

On 25th April the destination of the cup was finally settled. For the third time the clubs met at Celtic Park and Rangers ran out 2-0 winners.

FACT 23

1906
WINNING THE CUP EVERY FIVE YEARS

Hearts won their fourth Scottish Cup in 1905-06, keeping up a curious record of winning the competition every five years.

Just like in 1901, the final was played at Ibrox and again Hearts opponents were from Glasgow. This time they faced Third Lanark, who had won the competition the previous year.

The game was not an entertaining one, marred by the weather and Third Lanark's solid defensive tactics. George Wilson eventually broke the deadlock when he scored for Hearts with nine minutes remaining and it stayed 1-0 until full time.

The cup was presented after the game at the Alexandra Hotel. As he received it, Hearts chairman Robert Wilson said that it was a strange coincidence that they had won it every five years. He praised Third Lanark's sportsmanship in admitting that the best team won and said that it was good to see honours shared around.

When the team and officials arrived back in Edinburgh, they were greeted by scenes never witnessed for any of the previous three cup triumphs. Up to 30,000 fans gathered along Lothian Road and a band played 'See the Conquering Hero Comes'. There were deafening cheers as the party proceeded to the Imperial Hotel for a private reception.

FACT 24
1912
THE FIRST OVERSEAS TOUR

Hearts first games outside the British Isles were in May 1912, when they undertook a tour of Scandinavia.

The first game was on 12th May against Grenland Kretslag and attracted a crowd of 6,000 to the Frogner Stadium. The spectators included Norway's monarch, King Haakon, who had come specifically to see Bobby Walker and Hearts cruise to a 6-0 win.

Two days later Hearts played Kristiania Kretslag but there were no signs of fatigue as they thrashed their hosts 9-0, Percy Dawson scoring four.

The touring party then moved on to the Danish capital of Copenhagen. The country was in mourning following the sudden death of their monarch King Frederick VIII, brother of Britain's Queen Alexandra, on 15th May. As a mark of respect the game against a Copenhagen Select XI scheduled for the 17th was postponed by two days.

The Danes were far better than their Norwegian counterparts and Hearts had to come from behind to draw 1-1. On 21st May they met a select side again and won 2-0. Hearts then returned to Edinburgh as Denmark prepared for the funeral of their King which took place on the 25th.

FACT 25
1914
THE NEW MAIN STAND

Tynecastle's first Main Stand, which was demolished in 2017, had first been opened on 15th August 1914.

The stand was designed by renowned stadium architect Archibald Leitch. It could seat 4,000 fans with an enclosure in front and ran the length of the pitch. It replaced two smaller stands and a pavilion that had been on that side of the ground.

Part of the finances for the stand had come from the sale of centre forward Percy Dawson to Blackburn Rovers for a fee of £2,500. Hearts then paid Liverpool £400 for his replacement, Tom Gracie.

The stand opened with little fanfare. Britain had declared war on Germany eleven days earlier and two players who were army reservists had already been called up to the forces. On the opening day of the new season, Hearts welcomed champions Celtic to Tynecastle and won 2-0 in front of 18,000 spectators. Gracie scored the second goal eight minutes from time.

By the time the stand was completed in October, the projected cost had risen to over £12,000 which was twice what had been anticipated. This would place a great financial strain on the club during the war, in which Hearts led by example when it came to players joining up to fight.

FACT 26

1914
MCRAE'S BATTALION

In November 1914, sixteen Hearts players swapped the football field for the trenches. Britain had been at war with Germany for three months and Hearts was the first British club whose players enlisted en masse with the armed forces.

The regiment they joined, the 16th Royal Scots, is commonly known as McRae's Battalion, after their Colonel, George McRae. He was the M.P. for Edinburgh East. Other clubs followed the example of Hearts and their contingent was soon joined by seven players from Raith Rovers. After a period of training they were sent to the Western Front.

The bloodiest day of the First World War was the first day of the Battle of the Somme in July 1916. 20,000 British soldiers were killed, including three Hearts players. During the course of the war, the club lost seven players in the fighting. They were John Allan, James Boyd, Duncan Currie, Ernest Ellis, Tom Gracie, James Speedie and Henry Wattie.

The Hearts War Memorial is situated in Haymarket and was unveiled in 1922. This is close to the offices where the players enlisted for service. Every Remembrance Sunday players, officials and supporters gather there to pay their respects.

FACT 27
1919
SON REPLACES
DAD AS MANAGER

When John McCartney resigned as Hearts manager in October 1919, he was replaced in the role by his son Willie.

McCartney took over as Hearts manager in 1910. He developed a team of exciting young players who were top of the league when the players enlisted en masse for war service in November 1914. Hearts eventually finished second that season, four points behind Celtic.

In 1918 McCartney published a booklet called *The Hearts & The Great War*, paying tribute to those who made the ultimate sacrifice.

Hearts were sixth in the table when McCartney resigned, following disagreements with directors over player recruitment and team selection. News reports said that his resignation had been accepted with regret. He moved to England where he managed Portsmouth and Luton Town. He also published another booklet documenting all Scottish footballers in the war.

McCartney was surprisingly replaced by his son Willie. His playing career had been cut short by injury leading to him becoming a referee. He remained in charge until 1935 and although some attractive football was played, the only trophies he could deliver were local ones. He later managed Hibs.

FACT 28
1926
JOHN WHITE'S TRIPLE QUADRUPLE

In February 1926 Hearts striker Jock White scored four goals in three successive matches, a feat unequalled in British football.

White joined Hearts from Albion Rovers in 1922. He had played for them in the 1920 Scottish Cup final and remains the only Albion player to be capped by Scotland whilst there.

White's amazing goalscoring run started against Dundee United on Monday 1st February in a Scottish Cup first round replay at Tynecastle. Hearts won 6-0 with three of White's goals coming in the second half.

Five days later Hearts were back in cup action, welcoming Alloa to Tynecastle in the second round. White got two goals in each half as Hearts won 5-2 against a stubborn Alloa side, who had twice equalised before the break.

The following Wednesday, Hearts faced Hamilton Academical in the league at Tynecastle. White scored the only four goals of the game, three of them in the second half.

The next match was away at Airdrie. White was unable to continue the sequence, but the one goal he did score was still an important one, drawing Hearts level at 2-2 after falling behind to a penalty. No player has ever managed to succeed in repeating his remarkable goalscoring achievement in England or Scotland.

FACT 29
1931
HEARTS LEADING SCORER IN A SINGLE SEASON

In 1930-31 Barney Battles scored 44 league goals, the highest total in a single season by any Hearts player.

Battles was the son of another player of the same name who played sixteen games for Hearts in 1894-95 before moving to Celtic. In 1924 Battles Jnr emigrated to the United States and played for Boston in the American Soccer League, but returned to Scotland at the outset of the Great Depression in 1928, joining Hearts.

In his first season Battles made an instant impact, scoring 31 league goals in 28 games to set a new club scoring record. In 1929-30 he got a lower total of 26 in the league, but scored seven in the Scottish Cup, meaning his overall total was better than the season before.

In his record-breaking season, Battles scored hat-tricks in three successive games during November. His 44 goals were even more remarkable considering he only took part in 29 of the 38 games due to appendicitis. Hearts finished in fifth place, with Battles scoring 44 of their ninety goals.

Battles remained at Hearts until 1936 but injuries prevented him getting anywhere near his record breaking tally. After retiring from playing he worked as a physiotherapist, journalist and publican.

FACT 30
1932 RECORD ATTENDANCE

Tynecastle's record attendance is 53,396, for a Scottish Cup third round tie between Hearts with Rangers on 13th February 1932.

Hearts had comfortably beaten Lochgelly United and Cowdenbeath to reach the last sixteen of the competition. Rangers though were a different proposition, having won the Scottish League Championship for the last five seasons.

Supporters started queuing at 8am and ninety minutes before kick off all seats were taken and there were 20,000 inside the ground. The *Edinburgh Evening News* reported that the police acted as stewards "marshalling the gathering crowd closer together and the arrangements worked in fairly convincing fashion."

Despite the size of the crowd, it was not very noisy but the Rangers contingent had something to cheer for when they took the lead after sixteen minutes. Hearts had a chance to get back in it when they were awarded a penalty for handball but Alex Massie's kick was saved.

In the second half Hearts did their best to get back in the game but Rangers' defence remained strong. There could have been no complaints from Rangers however if Hearts had found an equaliser.

The attendance was initially published as 55,000 but eventually confirmed as 53,396. This beat the 51,000 who had turned out for a Scottish Cup tie with Celtic in 1926.

FACT 31
1935
HIGHEST SCORING EDINBURGH DERBY

The highest scoring Edinburgh derby was on 21st September 1935, when Hearts thrashed Hibs 8-3 at Tynecastle.

Hearts were clear favourites for a match against a Hibs side that hadn't won in their opening eight fixtures. However even the most optimistic of Hearts fans must have been surprised when they went 2-0 up in the first five minutes, both goals scored by Tommy Walker.

Andy Black scored a fine solo goal after twenty minutes then headed another to make it 4-0 just before half time. Hearts then started the second half as they had the first, scoring twice within five minutes through Charlie Wipfler and Alex Munro.

At 6-0 Hearts eased up and Hibs scored three goals in quick succession, causing some nerves among the crowd. However Wipfler produced some fine solo skill to score his second and end any hopes of a further Hibs comeback.

Towards the end of the game Dave McCulloch scored from close range to complete the rout. The 8-3 score line remains the highest ever in an Edinburgh derby and the only time Hearts have put eight goals past their city rivals.

FACT 32
1937
RECORD SCOTTISH CUP VICTORY

Hearts record victory in the Scottish Cup was on 13th February 1937. They thrashed King's Park 15-0 in the second round at Tynecastle, with Bill Walsh scoring eight of the goals.

A few days before this game King's Park; a side based in Stirling, had needed extra time to win their replay at Elgin City of the Highland League. Even allowing for these exertions though, the game was ridiculously one side considering King's Park were a Second Division side, albeit a struggling one.

The Scotsman reported that the King's Park players had shown "plucky defence" prior to conceding the first goal, scored by Walsh, after fourteen minutes. After that the floodgates well and truly opened and it was 9-0 by half time. Walsh had scored four of those goals, with Tommy Walker and Andy Black also grabbing two each.

Walsh scored the first four goals of the second half to take the score to 13-0. Freddie Warren and Jimmy Dykes completed the rout. The paper said that Hearts could have scored more but their forwards did not maintain full determination.

The victory was as good as it would get that season, as in the following round Hearts lost 2-1 at Hamilton Academical.

FACT 33

1940
THE
FOGGY DERBY

On 1st January 1940 Hearts beat Hibs 6-5 at a foggy Easter Road. For reasons of national security, the game could not be called off.

The outbreak of the Second World War led to the regionalisation of competitions. This fixture was in the East & North League but looked set to be postponed due to thick fog. However the War Office insisted it go ahead as they didn't want the enemy to be aware of the bad weather.

Commentator Bob Kingsley could only see the two wingers nearest the touchline closest to where he was sat. He had to rely on a runner to come and go between the pitch and his position to update him on goal scorers, while much of the commentary he simply made up as he went along.

Hearts trailed 3-2 at half time but hit back to win 6-5. Tommy Walker scored the winner in the last minute as darkness added to the confusion. Kingsley then continued commentating after the final whistle, while one Hearts player didn't even realise the game had finished and stayed out on the wing.

FACT 34

1948
THE
TERRIBLE TRIO

The most famous forward line in Hearts history played together for the first time on 9th October 1948. The 'Terrible Trio' of Alfie Conn, Jimmy Wardhaugh and Willie Bauld were all on the scoresheet as Hearts beat East Fife 6-1 in a Scottish League Cup group game.

Hearts were bottom of the league after six games and could not progress to the knockout stage of the League Cup. The game against the cup holders was thus an opportunity to experiment with the side and a debut was granted to Bauld, who had been on loan at Edinburgh City for two seasons.

Bauld made an instant impression, scoring a hat-trick in a 6-1 victory in which Conn also scored twice. The following week in another League Cup game at Queen of the South, Bauld got a hat-trick again as the trio played together in a 4-0 victory. In each game the opposition had no answer to Wardhaugh's dribbling ability, Bauld's aerial strength and Conn's strength and powerful shooting.

On 23rd October at Ibrox in a league game, manager David McLean maintained faith in his young forward line. Hearts beat Rangers 2-0, the goals coming from Wardhaugh and Conn. The Terrible Trio were there to stay and for the next nine years terrorised defences across Scotland.

FACT 35
1952
HEARTS TRIUMPH BEFORE RECORD DERBY CROWD

The highest ever crowd for an Edinburgh derby was on 2nd January 1950, when 65,860 fans packed into Easter Road. It was Hearts fans who went home happy as they saw their side come from behind to win 2-1.

Beforehand, newspapers billed the game as 'the classic of the season.' Hibs were top of the league, four points ahead of Hearts who had played a game more. Some of the record crowd forced entry and dozens were treated for fainting and crush injuries.

Hibs had the better of the first half and Gordon Smith headed them in front after half an hour. At half time Hearts were fortunate to be just the one goal behind.

Whatever was said in the dressing room, it fired up the Hearts players and they were transformed in the second half. Alfie Conn levelled the scores after seven minutes when he hit an unstoppable shot from twelve yards. From then on it was all Hearts and with twelve minutes left Jimmy Wardhaugh seized on a defensive error to take the ball and blast it past the keeper.

The victory was Hearts eleventh in succession and the following day they hammered St Mirren 5-0 at Tynecastle. However they lost two of the next three games and ended up finishing third, seven points behind champions Rangers.

FACT 36
1951
HIGHEST SCORING DRAW

The highest scoring drawn game that Hearts have been involved in was 5-5, against St Mirren in the Scottish League Cup on 18th August 1951.

This was the third game of the sectional stage, with Hearts having drawn one and lost one so far. They got off to a perfect start, Willie Bauld scoring after just twenty seconds midway through the first half Bauld had completed his hat-trick as Hearts led 3-1.

Despite St Mirren's keeper picking up an injury and swapping positions with one of their wingers, Hearts couldn't add to their tally before half time. Instead, the home side struck back through Alex Crowe with his second of the game and Alex Burrell.

Within five minutes of the restart Hearts had restored their two-goal advantage with Bauld getting both the goals. They could have been 6-3 ahead but Jimmy Wardhaugh's effort crashed back off the bar.

Hearts looked to be set for victory only for Crowe to score twice in a four-minute spell. In the dying seconds, St Mirren thought they should have been awarded a penalty when Burrell went down in the area but their claims were waved away.

The draw did neither side any good in the longer run, as it was Dundee who topped the group and progressed to the knockout stages.

FACT 37
1953
DAVE MACKAY'S DEBUT

Dave MacKay, arguably Hearts best-ever midfield player, made his debut on 3rd November 1953.

MacKay joined Hearts as a sixteen-year-old in 1951 but continued his joinery apprenticeship. He went on to gain Scottish junior international caps and became full time in the summer of 1953.

MacKay made his debut at wing half against Clyde at Tynecastle, a game Hearts lost 2-1. He became a regular in the side in 1954-55, soon tasting success in the Scottish League Cup and Scottish Cup before captaining Hearts to their title success in 1958.

Even when he was called up for National Service, MacKay continued to return from his bases in southern England to turn out for Hearts. He won his first Scottish cap in 1957 and was in the squad for the 1958 World Cup in Sweden.

MacKay was strong in the tackle, had boundless energy and was confident on the ball. He was never booked in any of his 208 games for Hearts, in which he scored 32 goals.

During 1958-59 MacKay was in and out of the side through injury, but this didn't stop Tottenham Hotspur launching a £32,000 bid in March 1959. Supporters were dismayed when this was accepted and MacKay went onto have a successful career in England, captaining Spurs to the Double in 1961.

FACT 38
1954
SCOTLAND'S FIRST ALL CONCRETE STADIUM

In the close season of 1954 the enclosure in front of Tynecastle's Main Stand was concreted. This meant that Hearts were the first team in Scotland to play in an all concrete stadium.

When the terracing at Tynecastle was expanded during the 1920s, the club used ash from the nearby Haymarket railway yards. Rows of railway sleepers gave fans something solid to stand on, although these could be slippery in the rain.

In 1951, three sides of the ground were covered with concrete at the cost of £16,500. Facilities were improved for players too, with the installation of dressing room showers.

For three years the Main Stand enclosure, which could accommodate 7,000, was the only part of the ground where the terracing was not concrete. This was rectified in the summer of 1954 and Tynecastle was the first all concrete stadium in Scotland.

Club architects stated the capacity of the improved ground was 54,000 but for big matches the club printed 5,000 fewer tickets for safety reasons. A further addition in November of 1954 was the painting of the club crest over the players' tunnel.

FACT 39

1954
END OF A
48 YEAR WAIT

On 23rd October 1954 Hearts beat Motherwell in the Scottish League Cup final to finally end their 48-year trophy drought.

In the group stage they won five of their six games then brushed aside St Johnstone 7-0 on aggregate in the quarter final. They then comfortably beat Airdrie 4-1 at Easter Road in the semi-final.

For the final against Motherwell, Hearts were slight favourites although the opposition had in their ranks some flair players who could pose a danger. A poor attendance was predicted, but there were over 55,000 in Hampden Park and the two sides played out arguably the most entertaining League Cup final to date.

Willie Bauld scored twice in the first sixteen minutes to put Hearts in control of the game. Five minutes before half time Willie Redpath pulled a goal back from the penalty spot after forty minutes but on the stroke of half time Jimmy Waurdhaugh restored Hearts two goal advantage.

Three minutes from time Bauld completed his hat-trick to make it 4-1 and seal victory for Hearts. Alex Bain scored a consolation for Motherwell in the last minute.

The victory was no more than Hearts deserved and was down to their guile and spirit. Fans celebrated long and hard as Hearts lifted their first trophy since winning the Scottish Cup back in 1906.

FACT 40

1956
A DREAM OF FIFTY YEARS

Hearts won the Scottish Cup in 1955-56, beating Celtic 3-1 in the final to win the competition for the first time in fifty years.

Despite dominating the first half in which the wind was in their favour, Hearts only led 1-0 at half time thanks to Ian Crawford's twentieth minute strike. Three minutes after the restart Crawford added another, firing home after a cross by Willie Bauld.

After 55 minutes, Hearts keeper Willie Duff dropped a free kick and Celtic's Mike Haughney prodded the ball into the net. This galvanised Celtic but Hearts refused to be overwhelmed, with MacKay rock solid in midfield. Hearts regained the upper hand and with ten minutes remaining Bauld was again involved in the build up to a goal, this time scored by Alfie Conn.

Later thousands of fans welcomed the jubilant Hearts players as they undertook a seven mile open top bus tour of the city before having a private celebration.

Hearts had undoubtedly deserved their victory, with *The Scotsman* correspondent concluding "I doubt if there ever has been a more popular result. Down the years Hearts have been welcome visitors at all grounds in Scotland, acclaimed for the skill and ability of their sides, yet always flattering to deceive."

FACT 41
1957
FLOODLIGHTS

Floodlights were installed at Tynecastle 1957, with city rivals Hibs being invited to play in a friendly to mark their switch on.

The system was installed at a cost of £15,000. There were four pylons, each 100 feet in height, with amps providing 2,000 watts of energy.

Despite the game against Hibs on 7th October being an exhibition match, there was no question of it not being taken seriously. Both clubs fielded strong sides and the game attracted a crowd of 25,000. News reports stated that the lights "gave an even illumination of every corner of the field with no shadows of any description."

Hearts raced into a two-goal lead midway through the first half through Willie Bauld and Jimmy Wardhaugh. However teenager Jimmy Preston pulled a goal back shortly before half an hour had been played. After the break Hearts were stunned as Preston got two more to complete a hat-trick and the game ended 4-2.

Later that month the lights were on again as Tynecastle hosted a Scotland Under 23 friendly, in which they beat Holland 4-1. Hearts hosted further friendlies during the season against Newcastle United, the British Army and a Scotland XI.

FACT 42
1958
HEARTS GREATEST EVER SEASON

In 1957-58 Hearts stormed to the Scottish First Division championship, scoring a record 132 goals.

Hearts were unbeaten in their first eleven games and never looked like missing out on the title. They lost just one game all season and finished with 62 points, thirteen ahead of second place Rangers.

Opposition defences had no answer to Hearts lethal attack. They failed to score just once, in a 0-0 draw at Third Lanark and hit four or more goals in a game on eighteen occasions. Jimmy Wardhaugh was the leading scorer with 37.

At Tynecastle, thrashings were handed out to East Fife (9-0), Falkirk (9-1) and Queens Park (8-0). The highest scoring away victory was 7-2 at Airdrie in the second game of the season.

Despite their huge advantage, Hearts were not confirmed as champions until they had just two games remaining. The reason for this is that Rangers had several games in hand. However a 3-2 win at St Mirren on 14th April ensured Hearts couldn't be caught even if Rangers won their last nine games.

In addition to the record breaking 132 goals, Hearts finished with a goal difference of +103, the only time a team has had more than +100 in the Scottish top division.

FACT 43
1958 EUROPEAN CLUB COMPETITION

Hearts took part in European competition for the first time in 1958-59 but were eliminated at the first hurdle.

In the preliminary round of the European Cup, Hearts were drawn against Belgian champions Standard Liege. In the first leg at the Sclessin Stadium on 3rd September, Ian Crawford gave Hearts a fourteenth minute lead but the Belgians drew level three minutes later through Jean Jadot. André Piters added another for the home side to leave Hearts trailing 2-1 at half time.

It remained that way until seventeen minutes from time when Paul Bonga-Bonga scored Standard's third. Denis Houf scored a fourth and Jadot got another to complete a 5-1 rout leaving Hearts with a mountain to climb in the second leg.

Six days later at Tynecastle, Standard were content to sit back and defend. Willie Bauld finally broke the deadlock after 55 minutes only for Joseph Givard to equalise three minutes later. Bauld restored Hearts lead after 63 minutes and Hearts continued to press but couldn't find the additional goals they needed.

Press reports described it as a "tough game, unsuited to the atmosphere of the European Cup" but added that the French referee did well to keep it under control.

FACT 44
1958
NO BAD LUCK IN
13TH LEAGUE CUP FINAL

Hearts reached the final of the thirteenth Scottish League Cup competition. However there was no bad luck as they cruised to a 5-1 victory over Partick Thistle.

In the group stage, Hearts overcame a 3-0 defeat in their opening fixture against Rangers at Ibrox to win the remaining five matches. They secured qualification with a game to spare, beating Third Lanark 5-4 in a thrilling game at Cathkin Park.

Hearts comfortably beat Ayr United over two legs in the quarter final. A 5-1 win at Somerset Park was followed up with a 3-1 victory at Tynecastle. They then played some glorious football against Kilmarnock in the semi-final, winning 3-0 at Easter Road.

The final against Partick, who had shocked Celtic in the other semi-final, was played on 25th October. Hearts were 2-0 up after just ten minutes thanks to goals from Willie Bauld and Jimmy Murray. Both players scored again to give them a comfortable 4-0 half time lead.

Partick pulled a goal back straight from the restart but any Hearts nerves about an unlikely comeback were settled after an hour when Johnny Hamilton scored their fifth.

FACT 45
1959
AUSTRALIA

After the end of the 1958-59 season, Hearts became the first Scottish team to tour Australia.

After a successful tour of Canada in 1958, Hearts looked to venture even further in 1959. They agreed to play fifteen games and a party of sixteen players, two coaching staff and two directors left Prestwick Airport on 2nd May. They had several stopovers before arriving in Sydney four days later.

The players were allowed a few days rest before their opening game, a 7-1 win against the Australian national side on 9th May. The following day they played an Australia XI in Sydney, winning 6-1. They then flew north to Brisbane for two games, a 3-2 draw with Queensland and 7-1 win over Australia.

They then returned to New South Wales for three more games, which were all comfortably won, before moving on to Melbourne which had hosted the 1956 Olympics. Hearts won 9-1 and 5-0 against Australia and Victoria respectively. Next stop was the island state of Tasmania, where they recorded their biggest win of the tour, 10-0.

Victoria requested another game so Hearts returned to Melbourne and beat them 7-1. They beat South Australia 8-0 in Adelaide before flying west to Perth. They won 9-0 against Australia and 10-1 against Western Australia. The party finally arrived back in Scotland on 19th June.

FACT 46

1960
LEAGUE AND
LEAGUE CUP DOUBLE

In 1959-60 Hearts won the Scottish League Championship and Scottish League Cup. They remain the only club apart from the Old Firm to win these two trophies in the same season.

In the League Cup final on 24th October 1959, Hearts fell behind to Third Lanark after just two minutes. However second half goals from Johnny Hamilton and Alex Young gave Hearts a 2-1 win and they retained the trophy.

Four days after the cup final, Hearts met Third Lanark again in a league game at Tynecastle and won 6-2 to maintain their unbeaten start to the season. They didn't lose until their fifteenth game, when St Mirren won 2-0 at Tynecastle.

Hearts lost only three times all season, with Alex Young ending up as the leading scorer with 28 goals. They clinched the Championship in their penultimate game away to St Mirren. In a thrilling contest, Hearts came from behind on four occasions to draw 4-4, with Willie Bauld getting the decisive goal just a minute from time

It was Hearts fourth Championship, but they haven't won the title since. No other club apart from the Old Firm of Rangers and Celtic have won the Championship and League Cup in the same season.

FACT 47
1960
ALEX YOUNG DEPARTS

In November 1960 a striker who had played a key part in Hearts success in recent years was sold to Everton, where he earned the nickname Golden Vision.

Alex Young made his debut for Hearts in 1955 as an eighteen-year-old. In 1957-58 he was part of the forward line that scored an astonishing 132 goals on their way to the title. Blessed with acceleration, a strong shot and heading ability, he scored the clinching goal in a 3-2 win at St Mirren which confirmed Hearts as champions.

In 1959-60 Young scored the winning goal in the League Cup final and 23 goals in the First Division as Hearts won the title again. The highlight of his league season was a hat-trick in a 5-1 win over Hibs at Easter Road.

When Everton made a combined bid of £55,000 for Young and George Thomson, Hearts were unable to refuse the offer. He left Tynecastle having scored 103 goals in 193 appearances.

Young went on to become a legend at Goodison Park, where fans dubbed him the 'Golden Vision.' After retiring from playing he returned to Edinburgh and ran an upholstery business. He was inducted into the Hearts Hall of Fame in 2007.

FACT 48
1961
SCHOOL STUDIES COME FIRST

When Hearts played a European tie in Italy in November 1961, one of their forwards was missing as he couldn't take time off school.

Seventeen-year-old Alan Gordon was a pupil at George Heriot's School but after thirteen goals in just eight reserve games he was called up to the first team in October 1961. He made his debut against Celtic at Tynecastle and then played against Rangers in the League Cup final at Hampden Park.

Hearts were 1-0 down from the first leg of the Inter Cities Fairs Cup second round tie against Inter Milan. However Gordon was unavailable for the return leg in the San Siro Stadium on 22nd November. He had hopes of going on to university to study economics and as such football had to take second place.

Inter comfortably progressed after winning the game 4-0. Three days later Gordon was back in the side and scored the decisive goal in a 1-0 win at Raith Rovers.

Gordon continued to combine football and studies after qualifying as an accountant. He left Hearts in 1967 for a spell in South Africa but was back the following year before joining Dundee United in 1969. He also played for Hibs and Dundee, making him the only player to play for both major Edinburgh and Dundee clubs.

FACT 49
1962 LEAGUE CUP WINNERS

Hearts won the League Cup in 1962-63, beating Kilmarnock in the final on 27th October 1962.

After topping a group that also included Celtic, Hearts comfortably beat Morton 6-1 on aggregate in the quarter finals. They then beat St Johnstone 4-0 in the semi-final at Easter Road to set up a final with Kilmarnock.

In front of 51,000 fans at Hampden Park, Norrie Davidson put Hearts ahead in the 25th minute when he converted Willie Hamilton's cross. It was the only goal of the game and secured Hearts seventh trophy in nine seasons.

Decades later, Davidson was in a pub when he heard two men arguing over who had scored the winning goal in this final and he was happy to settle the argument.

Amongst the crowd that day was future Scottish First Minister Alex Salmond. He later recalled that he was hoisted onto his father's shoulders to see the cup being lifted by captain John Cummings and promised it would be the first of many he'd see. It would be another three decades before they won another trophy and they have not won the League Cup since.

FACT 50
1963
HEARTS OUT AFTER MARATHON EURO TIE

In 1963-64 Hearts were knocked out of the Inter Cities Fairs Cup by Lausanne. The Swiss side finally claimed victory in extra time of a play off after the sides couldn't be separated over two legs.

In the first leg at the Olympique de la Pontaise, Hearts let a two-goal lead slip in a 2-2 draw. At a rain swept Tynecastle, Lausanne shocked Hearts when they fought back from a goal down to take a 2-1 lead with just two minutes remaining. Johnny Hamilton headed a last gasp equaliser but there was no extra time or penalties then and a third game would be necessary to settle the tie.

Hearts lost the toss over the venue meaning the sides met again in Lausanne six days later, on 15th October. Hearts were two down after twenty minutes, but Willie Wallace scored after half an hour to give them hope.

The second half was dominated by Hearts and they deservedly drew level with a Danny Ferguson goal on 65 minutes. Hearts dominated the rest of the game but poor finishing and goalkeeping heroics denied them a winner. At the other end Lausanne didn't have a single shot in the second half.

Eight minutes into the first period of extra time Heinz Schneiter scored for Lausanne and Hearts couldn't find a way back.

FACT 51

1964
ROALD JENSEN

The first player from outside the British Isles to play for Hearts was Norwegian Roald Jensen, who joined the club in December 1964.

The 21-year-old winger had twice been named Norwegian footballer of the year whilst playing for Brann Bergen. Noted for his shooting and crossing accuracy, he initially joined Hearts as an amateur whilst studying textile engineering in Edinburgh.

Jensen made his debut on 2nd January 1965 in a 3-2 defeat at Dunfermline. Three weeks later he scored the only goal of the game as Hearts beat Partick Thistle 1-0 at Tynecastle.

After opting to stay in Scotland and signing as a professional, Jensen remained with Hearts until 1971. However he regularly had to battle injuries and was limited to 101 appearances in all competitions, scoring 25 goals.

In 1971 Jensen returned to Norway and re-joined Brann, being named Norwegian footballer of the year on two more occasions. He retired from playing two years later, although did make a guest appearance for Hearts in a friendly against his old club in 1976. He died suddenly in 1987 aged just 44 and there is a statue of him outside Brann's stadium.

FACT 52
1965
DENIED TITLE BY
0.042 OF A GOAL

In one of the closest ever finishes to a season, Hearts lost on the last day of 1964-65 to Kilmarnock, who pipped them to the title on goal average.

Hearts led Killie at the top by two points going into the game at Tynecastle on 24th April. A point or defeat by one goal would be enough to secure the title, but a two-goal loss would see Killie finish as champions.

There was no question of Hearts sitting back for the point and Roald Jensen hit the post after five minutes. In an end to end game, Hearts fell behind after 27 minutes when David Sneddon headed in Tommy McLean's cross. Just two minutes later, Brian McIlroy's low drive made it 2-0.

For the next hour Hearts did all they could to find the crucial goal. They came close when Roy Barry headed over the bar then in injury time his shot was agonisingly turned round the post by the keeper.

When the full-time whistle blew, it meant Hearts had lost out on the title by 0.042 of a goal. It was Killie's first title after finishing runners up in four out of the last five seasons. Had goal difference been used to determine placings, Hearts would have been champions, as theirs was +41 to Killie's +29.

FACT 53
1967
THE IRON MAN LEAVES

John Cumming, Hearts most decorated player, spent his entire playing career with the club prior to retiring in 1967.

A former pit worker, Cumming played for Hearts youth side but didn't sign as a full time professional until January 1950 when he was nineteen years old. Appearances were sporadic for three years and it was not until 1953-54 that he became a regular in the side. His versatility meant he was equally comfortable on the left side of midfield and defence.

Cumming earned the nickname the 'Iron Man' due to his fearless tackling. However he was always fair and was never booked in any of the 500+ appearances he made for Hearts. In the 1956 Scottish Cup final against Celtic, he had a clash of heads with Willie Fernie but returned to the field and was named man of the match.

Between 1954 and 1962 Hearts won seven major trophies. Cumming was the only player to play in both title winning sides and also all five cup finals. He was capped nine times by Scotland.

After making just two appearances in 1966-67, Cumming retired from playing but remained at Tynecastle on the coaching staff for nine years. In 1980 he was granted a testimonial, a game that saw an Edinburgh Select XI play a North East England XI.

FACT 54
1967
JIM CRUICKSHANK'S
TRIPLE PENALTY SAVE

Hearts keeper Jim Cruickshank played one of his best ever games to ensure they avoided defeat against Hibs on 2nd January 1967. The highlight of the game was when he saved a penalty and both follow up attempts.

Hibs had more of the play in a bruising encounter that too often saw Hearts resorting to fouls to break up the visitors' attacks. Five minutes before half time the referee had finally seen enough and booked eighteen-year-old defender Arthur Thomson for a bad challenge on Jimmy O'Rourke.

Four minutes into the second half Alan MacDonald fouled Eric Stevenson in the area and Hibs were awarded a penalty. Joe Davis took the kick but Cruickshank guessed right and dived to make the save. Davis followed up but the Hearts keeper again blocked his effort. He then recovered to smother the ball as Allan McGraw pounced.

Cruickshank's heroics galvanised Hearts and Davie Holt almost scored but his header bounced off the bar. Hibs then regained the upper hand and Cruickshank made two world class saves from O'Rourke. The game finished 0-0 and Hearts had Cruickshank to thank for picking up a point.

FACT 55
1967
RECORD POST WAR LOW CROWD

The lowest crowd to watch a league match at Tynecastle since the Second World War was on 19th April 1967, when just 1,846 turned up for a game against Stirling Albion.

Hearts were on a dismal run of eight games without a win. Seven of these games were lost and they had scored just two goals. They had slumped to thirteenth in the table, three places above Stirling.

Eighteen-year-old Andy Milne was given another opportunity, having made his debut the previous month. He scored two goals within a minute midway through the first half to give Hearts a 2-0 lead at the break. Four minutes after the restart he completed his hat-trick and almost got a fourth but his effort hit the post.

Stirling pulled a goal back in the 62nd minute but within two minutes Bobby Kemp had restored Hearts three goal advantage. Jim Murphy scored the fifth twelve minutes from time. It was a game that reports said Hearts won comfortably without necessarily playing very well.

The attendance of 1,846 was one of only two occasions since the Second World War that Hearts have had a home crowd of less than 2,000. The other was in April 1981 when 1,866 attended a Premier League game with Kilmarnock.

FACT 56
1969
OUT ON
GOAL DIFFERENCE

In 1969 Hearts became the first team in Scotland to be disadvantaged by goal difference when they were eliminated from the group stage of the Scottish league Cup.

After losing out on the league to goal average in 1965, Hearts lobbied for a change to goal difference. This was eventually introduced by the Scottish League for the 1971-72 season.

However when Hearts and Morton finished level on points at the top of their League Cup group in August 1969, both teams had a goal average of 1:500. Goal difference was then used to determine the group winners meaning that Morton progressed due to having +3 compared to Hearts +2.

Had the head to head results of the two teams been used then Hearts would have progressed. When the teams met at Tynecastle Morton won 1-0, but at Cappielow it was Hearts who triumphed 2-0. This was actually on the last matchday and one more goal would have taken Hearts through.

Morton then went out in unusual fashion themselves in the quarter final. They beat Motherwell 3-0 at home in the first leg then lost the second by the same score line. A third game was then played, which Motherwell won 1-0 to progress.

FACT 57
1971 TEXACO CUP FINALISTS

In 1970-71 Hearts were beaten finalists in one of the world's first sponsored football competitions.

The International League Board Competition was open to clubs from England, Scotland, Northern Ireland and the Republic of Ireland who had not qualified for European competition. It became known as the Texaco Cup when the petroleum giant offered £100,000 in sponsorship.

Hearts were one of six Scottish sides to take part in the inaugural tournament, which was played on a straight knockout basis. In the first round against Burnley they overturned a 3-1 deficit to win 4-1 at Tynecastle in the second leg.

In the quarter and semi-finals, Hearts overcame Scottish opposition in Airdrie and Motherwell. This set up a two legged final with English First Division side Wolverhampton Wanderers.

In front of 25,027 fans at Tynecastle, Donald Ford gave Hearts a seventh minute lead but Wolves hit back to win 3-1. At Molineux, George Fleming scored for Hearts after 25 minutes but they were unable to add to this and Wolves held on to claim the trophy.

Hearts competed in the Texaco Cup for each of the next four seasons that it remained in existence, but never again managed to get past the quarter final stage.

FACT 58

1973 NEW YEAR DERBY WOE

Hearts' dismal run against Hibs continued in the worst possible fashion on 1st January 1973, when they suffered a humiliating 7-0 home defeat to their city rivals.

Going into this game Hearts hadn't beaten Hibs in the previous thirteen meetings, failing to score in the last nine of them. Hearts had lost their last two games and Hibs were challenging Celtic at the top of the league, but nobody could have foreseen what unfolded at Tynecastle that day.

Tommy Murray and Donald Park both missed early chances for Hearts. They were punished for this when Jimmy O'Rourke put the visitors ahead after nine minutes. For the rest of the first half Hearts defence offered little resistance against Hibs fast movement and by half time it was 5-0.

Eleven minutes into the second half Alan O'Rourke made it 6-0 and with a quarter of an hour remaining Alan Gordon completed his hat-trick when he got the seventh. Only some outstanding goalkeeping from Kenny Garland prevented the score line reaching double figures.

The 7-0 score line remains the biggest margin of victory in an Edinburgh derby. However, Hearts fans can still claim to have scored the most goals in a single game between the sides, referring to the 8-3 win in 1935.

FACT 59
1973
DONALD FORD'S
HAT TRICK OF PENALTIES

On 1st September 1973, Hearts came from two goals down to win 3-2 at Morton, with all three goals scored from the penalty spot by Donald Ford.

Morton took the lead after half an hour at Cappielow, then nine minutes into the second half went 2-0 up. Within three minutes Ford had pulled one back with a penalty, striking the ball low to the keeper's left to give Hearts hope of a comeback.

When Hearts were awarded another penalty in the 65th minute Ford opted to go for the other corner. The keeper did the same and almost got to the ball but it just crept in and the scores were level.

With ten minutes remaining Hearts were awarded another kick. This time the Morton players surrounded the referee, so sure were they that no team could ever be awarded three penalties in such a short space of time.

Ford has always maintained however that all three claims were genuine. He made no mistake, reverting to his usual practice of taking his kick hard and low to the keepers left to win the game for Hearts. It was another 37 years before there was another hat-trick of penalties in the top-flight when Paul Hartley scored three for Aberdeen against Hamilton.

FACT 60

1975
THE SCOTTISH PREMIER LEAGUE

Hearts were one of the ten teams that made up the Scottish Premier League in 1975 but were beaten in their opening fixture at Hibs.

In the summer of 1974 the 38 league clubs decided to end the two division 18-20 structure and move to a three tier model of 10-14-14. It meant that the top ten teams in the First Division in 1974-75 would make up the new Premier Division. Hearts finished in eighth place; four points clear of Airdrie in eleventh.

To ensure maximum impact of the new ten team league, it was decided that Glasgow and Edinburgh derbies would take place on the opening day. On 30th August Rangers played Celtic at Ibrox while Hearts crossed the Capital to take on Hibs at Easter Road.

Hearts got their season off to an uninspiring start. *The Scotsman* described them as "like a man in a boiler suit at a Royal garden party — completely out of place." Hibs won 1-0 to continue Hearts miserable run of failing to win there for seven years.

The following week Hearts lost 2-0 at home to Rangers, before getting off the mark in their third game, winning 3-2 at Dundee. They went on to finish in fifth place.

FACT 61
1976
A MEMORABLE EUROPEAN COMEBACK

One of the greatest European nights at Tynecastle was on 29th September 1976 when Hearts overturned a 2-0 first leg deficit to beat Lokomotiv Leipzig 5-1 in the Cup Winners Cup.

Hearts qualified for Europe despite losing the Scottish Cup final, as winners Celtic had done the Double so went into the European Cup. They were given a tough tie though and lost the first leg 2-0 in East Germany.

In a frenzied atmosphere at Tynecastle, Roy Kay opened the scoring after twelve minutes with a low drive and Willie Gibson made it 2-0 shortly before the half hour mark.

Lokomotiv scored a crucial away goal four minutes before half time, meaning Hearts needed two more. In the second half substitute Jim Shaw made an immediate impact, having a header cleared off the line and hitting the post with a shot.

After half an hour of the second period. two goals in the space of a minute sent the home fans wild. Jim Brown chipped the keeper and then Drew Busby scored after a flick on by Shaw. The Germans were demoralised and with four minutes remaining Gibson made it 5-1 with a fine headed goal.

Hearts faced West German opposition in the next round but were comfortably beaten 8-3 on aggregate by Hamburg, the eventual competition winners.

FACT 62
1977
RELEGATED FOR THE FIRST TIME

In 1976-77 Hearts finished ninth in the Premier League, meaning they were relegated for the first time in their history.

Hearts failed to win any of their first nine games, drawing seven and losing two. Too many draws would eventually prove their downfall, with Hearts winning just seven games all season and sixteen of the 36 fixtures ending all square.

On 5th February Hearts beat bottom side Kilmarnock 4-0 at Tynecastle, with all the goals coming in the first half. This lifted them up to fifth in the table and they appeared to be in no imminent danger of going down.

However, Hearts dropped into the bottom two during a dreadful run of twelve games without a win. At already relegated Kilmarnock on 16th April, Hearts trailed 2-0 at half time but fought back to draw 2-2. They now needed to win their remaining three games to stay up, and hope Motherwell lost all their remaining fixtures.

Hearts didn't have long to wait for their fate to be sealed, as the following day Motherwell beat Dundee United 4-0. Manager John Hagart was sacked a few days later and although Hearts would bounce straight back, the next six years were yo-yo ones.

FACT 63
1978
PROMOTED AT THE SEASIDE

Hearts won promotion back to the Premier League in 1977-78, after a run of 25 games was enough to edge out Dundee to the second promotion place.

Hearts were unbeaten in their first eight games, but then suffered five defeats from their next nine. However, a 2-0 defeat at East Fife on 12th November 1977 proved to be their last of the season.

Despite putting together a tremendous unbeaten run of 24 games, Hearts were still not sure of promotion by the last week of the season. Morton were already promoted as champions and Hearts knew they could only be certain of joining them by winning at Arbroath on 29th April 1978. Dundee were ready to pounce if Hearts slipped, although they did have a tough game at Morton.

Hearts were allocated 6,000 of 9,000 available tickets for the game at Gayfield Park, which was situated next to the North Sea. Eamonn Bannon headed Hearts in front after eighteen minutes and they held on for victory against an Arbroath side determined to avoid a repeat of the 7-0 score line when the sides met there earlier in the season.

There were joyous scenes at the final whistle and manager Willie Ormond, a former Hibs player, had now won the fans over after initial concerns at his appointment.

FACT 64

1978
A DEBUT GOAL IN FIFTY SECONDS

On 21st October 1978 Hearts new signing Derek O'Connor got off to a perfect start when he scored with his first touch on his debut at Aberdeen.

O'Connor was signed for £25,000 from St Johnstone and went straight into the side for this game at Pittodrie. After just fifty seconds, Hearts were awarded a free kick which was taken by Eamonn Bannon. O'Connor seized on defensive hesitation to reach the ball first, stabbing it into the net past despairing keeper Jim Leighton.

After fifteen minutes O'Connor almost doubled the lead but his header went just over the bar. Despite the Dons equalising from the penalty spot after an hour, substitute Denis McQuade scored the winner for Hearts eleven minutes from time with a long-range strike. It was only their second win of the season in the tenth game.

Amazingly O'Connor then returned to work as a draughtsman, his employer having insisted he work out his four-week notice. Working and training did not harm him though and two weeks later O'Connor was on target in the derby at Easter Road, scoring the second goal in a 2-1 victory. He remained at Tynecastle until 1984, scoring 47 league goals in 127 appearances.

FACT 65

1979 DOWN AGAIN

Hearts second visit of the season to Pittodrie in 1978-79 wasn't as memorable as the first. Aberdeen won 5-0 to condemn them to a seventh successive defeat and confirm their relegation back to the First Division.

In a season of struggle, Hearts spent just one week outside of the relegation places. However when they beat Motherwell 3-0 on 7th April survival was very much in their hands. With ten games to go they were two points behind Partick Thistle, who they still had to play twice.

Four days later Hearts suffered a crushing blow, losing 2-0 to Partick at Tynecastle. This was the first of ten successive defeats that brought a miserable season to a close.

Relegation was as good as confirmed with a 4-0 loss to Rangers at Ibrox on 28th April. Staying up was mathematically possible, but only if Hearts won their last four games, Partick lost theirs and there was a massive swing in goal difference.

At Pittodrie on 2nd May, manager Willie Ormond didn't even attend, preferring to scout new players instead for the following season's promotion push. The home side cruised to a 5-0 victory, with the *Aberdeen Evening Express* commenting that "This once mighty club is surely in its most depressed ever state."

1980
FACT 66 — MANAGER SACKED ON WAY TO PROMOTION

Willie Ormond was sacked as Hearts manager on 8th January 1980 even though they were top of the First Division. Despite this upheaval, they still went up as champions.

Hearts won their first five games of the season and at Hogmanay were second in the table. They were a point behind Dumbarton but with a game in hand on the leaders, as well as the three sides below them.

On 5th January Hearts let a three-goal lead slip at home to Clydebank, who scored all their goals in the last seventeen minutes to come back and draw 3-3. Three days later Ormond was sacked, the club issuing a seventeen-word statement offering little explanation as to why.

Bobby Moncur was appointed in the middle of February and the former Scottish international won four of his first five games in charge. This ensured promotion remained firmly in Hearts hands.

A spate of earlier postponements meant Hearts had to play nine league games in April. One of these was against Berwick Rangers, a game originally meant to be played on 1st January.

Hearts trailed 1-0 at half time but two minutes after the restart Frank Liddell equalised and the game finished 1-1. Hearts had clinched promotion with two games to spare, both of which were won to ensure they went up as champions.

FACT 67

1981
RELEGATED AS
APRIL FOOLS

Hearts were relegated for the third time in 1980-81 as they finished bottom of the Scottish Premier League. Relegation was confirmed on 1st April when they were beaten 6-0 at Celtic.

After losing their opening two games, Hearts hoped to have turned the tide after winning successive away games at St Mirren and Kilmarnock. However they then failed to win any of their next eleven games, a run that extended for three months.

The miserable sequence finally ended on 6th December with a 2-0 win over Kilmarnock, who were in an even more hopeless position than Hearts. There then followed a run of ten games without a win, eight of them defeats.

A 6-0 defeat to title chasing Celtic sealed Hearts fate with five games remaining. Four days later, just 1,866 turned up at Tynecastle to see Hearts beat Kilmarnock 1-0, a result that confirmed the Ayrshire side would be joining them in the First Division.

During the close season Edinburgh businessman Wallace Mercer took control of the club amidst a financial crisis that could have seen a move to players being part time. Bobby Moncur resigned as manager and after an audacious bid to lure Jim McLean from Dundee United failed, Moncur's assistant Tony Ford was appointed.

FACT 68
1982
THROWING PROMOTION AWAY

Hearts missed out on promotion straight back to the Scottish Premier League in 1981-82. They managed just one point from their last three games allowing Kilmarnock to grab second place.

Tony Ford was dismissed in December after a run of just one win in eight games. Alex MacDonald replaced him and after losing his first match in charge, won four in succession.

With three games remaining, Motherwell were already up as champions. Hearts were second, three points ahead of Kilmarnock, the only side who could overhaul them.

On 1st May Hearts led 2-1 at half time against Dumbarton at Tynecastle, only to concede four after the break and lose 5-2. On the same day, Kilmarnock won 5-1 at East Stirling to narrow the game to one point.

The following week Hearts and Kilmarnock faced each other at Rugby Park. A bad-tempered game finished 0-0 with few chances on either side. Both teams were reduced to ten men in the second half after an off the ball incident involving Gerry McCoy and Keith Robin.

Hearts now needed to beat Motherwell on the final day to guarantee promotion. They could still go up with a draw providing Kilmarnock didn't beat Queen of the South by five goals. Hearts lost 1-0, while Kilmarnock won 6-0, condemning them to another year in the First Division.

FACT 69
1983
BACK TO
THE PREMIER LEAGUE

Hearts made no mistake of securing promotion in 1982-83. There was the added satisfaction of sealing their return to the Scottish Premier League at the ground of the team that had shocked them at Tynecastle the previous season.

Hearts lost just twice before Christmas and on 1st January 1983 over 14,000 fans saw them beat leaders St Johnstone 1-0 at Tynecastle. This moved them to within a point of the top and opened up a four-point gap over Clydebank.

John Robertson was the leading scorer with 21 goals from just 23 appearances, including hat-tricks against Queens Park, Dunfermline and Partick Thistle. Fellow forward Derek O'Connor was an ever present in the side and netted sixteen times.

On 7th May Hearts travelled to Dumbarton, the side whose shock 5-2 win at Tynecastle the previous season had triggered the collapse that saw them miss out on promotion. This time Hearts made no mistake and cruised to a 4-0 victory to effectively secure promotion. With one game to go they were two points clear of Clydebank, but fifteen better off in terms of goal difference.

The following week Hearts made sure with a 2-0 win over Hamilton at Tynecastle to secure a return to the Scottish Premier League. This time they would not be coming straight back down.

FACT 70
1986
BROKEN HEARTED

In 1985-86 Hearts looked set for the Double, only to lose their last two games of the season and end up with nothing.

On the last weekend of September Hearts lost 1-0 at Clydebank to record a fifth defeat from the opening eight games. However Alan MacDonald's collection of bargain buys, youth and experience embarked on an astonishing run of 31 league and cup games unbeaten.

On 3rd May, Hearts needed just a point at Dundee to secure a first league title since 1960. Their 15,000 fans at Dens Park were dismayed when a penalty appeal was turned down after Sandy Clark went down in the box. At half time it was 0-0, but second placed Celtic were 4-0 up at St Mirren.

Celtic added another in the second half meaning they now had a superior goal difference, but with eight minutes remaining the title was still within Heart's grasp. However from a corner kick substitute Albert Kidd put Dundee 1-0 ahead and he added another in the last minute to shatter Hearts dreams.

A week later Hearts had the chance to salvage something from the season when they faced Aberdeen in the Scottish Cup final. Their confidence was sapped and they lost 3-0 to end the season trophyless.

FACT 71
1988
JOHN ROBERTSON'S
NINE MONTHS AWAY

John Robertson, Hearts all-time leading league goal scorer, may not have achieved this record had his move to Newcastle proved successful in 1988.

Robertson broke into the Hearts side as an eighteen-year-old and his 21 goals in 1982-83 helped them to promotion. He was not daunted by the step up to the Premier League and scored twenty goals in 1985-86 as Hearts just missed out on winning the title.

In April 1988, after 106 league goals for Hearts, he signed for Newcastle United. However in fourteen appearances he failed to score, and Hearts paid £750,000 to bring him back to Tynecastle in December of that year. Despite him not scoring at Newcastle, the English First Division club still made a £125,000 profit on the deal.

Robertson remained at Hearts until 1998. His final goals tally was 271 from 559 appearances in all competitions, including 214 in the league. 27 of these were against Hibs, earning him the nickname 'Hammer of Hibs.'

After finishing his playing career with Dundee and Livingston, Robertson went into management and was appointed as Hearts boss in November 2004. He was sacked after six months in charge despite finishing fifth in the league and reaching the semi-final of the Scottish Cup.

FACT 72
1989 UEFA CUP QUARTER FINALISTS

Hearts' best-ever run in European competition was 1988-89. They reached the quarter finals of the UEFA Cup and gave German giants Bayern Munich an almighty scare.

In the first round Hearts overcame Ireland's St Patrick's Athletic 4-0 on aggregate. They then faced Austria Vienna, drawing 0-0 at Tynecastle and winning 1-0 away. In the last sixteen they built a commanding 3-0 first leg lead against Velez Mostar of Yugoslavia, meaning the 2-1 away defeat ensured progress.

Hearts were then given a tough quarter final tie against Bayern Munich, champions of Europe three times in the 1970s. On 28th February the pitch at Tynecastle was a quagmire. The visitors struggled to come to terms with this and the raucous atmosphere generated by a crowd of 26,294. After 55 minutes home fans were sent into raptures when Iain Ferguson scored with a 25-yard thunderbolt to give Hearts a narrow lead to take to Munich.

In the second leg Hearts fell behind after fifteen minutes. However they didn't buckle and wouldn't let Bayern settle on the ball. There was agony midway through the second half when John Colquhoun's header glanced off the post. In the 69th minute Bayern scored again and Hearts were unable to find the all-important away goal. The travelling fans though were proud of their efforts.

FACT 73
1990 HIBS TAKEOVER ATTEMPT

In the summer of 1990, Hearts chairman Wallace Mercer made an audacious attempt to merge the club with Hibs to take on Glasgow's Old Firm.

Mercer reasoned that the only way the dominance of Celtic and Rangers could be challenged was if there were just one 'superclub' in Edinburgh. With Hibs in financial trouble, it was seen as more of a takeover however and their fans quickly rallied to oppose the sale.

There were demonstrations in Princes Street and Mercer received death threats from angry fans. One man was even found near his home with an axe. With shareholders refusing to sell to him, Mercer eventually withdrew his bid and Hibs were taken over by Kwik Fit owner Tom Farmer.

When Mercer died in January 2006, Hearts next game was against Hibs at Tynecastle. A one-minute applause was held by home fans for a chairman who had turned Hearts fortunes around, with Hibs fans turning their backs.

Mercer made his fortune from property development and had admitted that he misjudged the situation, especially in respect of football tribalism. However some members of his family have pointed to the Old Firms virtual monopoly of trophies since 1990 as vindication of his plans.

FACT 74

1994
22 DERBIES
UNBEATEN

During the 1993-94 season Hearts were unbeaten in the four league derbies with Hibs and also beat them in the Scottish Cup. It maintained a record of 22 games unbeaten in the Edinburgh derby.

Hibs beat Hearts 1-0 on 4th January 1989, but Hearts won the last encounter of that season 2-1 at Tynecastle. For each of the next two seasons Hearts won three and drew one, including impressive 3-0 and 4-1 wins at Easter Road in 1990-91.

In 1991-92 the first three derbies were drawn, with Hearts winning the fourth 2-1 at Easter Road. The following season both games at Hibs were drawn, with Hearts winning the two at Tynecastle.

Hearts won the first derby of 1993-94 1-0 at Tynecastle, then won 2-1 at Easter Road. The third derby of the season was a 1-1 draw at Tynecastle. The two sides met in February in the Scottish Cup fourth round. Hibs had home advantage but Hearts came away with a 2-1 victory. At the end of April, they drew 0-0 at Easter Road to make it 22 games unbeaten, 21 of them in the league.

The run finally came to an end in Hearts first home game of 1994-95, when Gordon Hunter's goal after an hour gave Hibs a 1-0 win.

FACT 75
1995
'THE ANIMAL' SIGNS FOR HEARTS

In 1995 Hearts signed Italian veteran Pasquale Bruno. The tough tackling defender nicknamed 'The Animal' in his homeland, soon became a cult figure among the Tynecastle faithful.

Bruno was 33 years old and had played in Serie A for Juventus, Torino and Lazio. He soon brought composure and leadership to a team that had struggled before his arrival. He made his debut on 4th November in a 3-0 home win over Partick Thistle that lifted the Jambos off the bottom of the table.

Hearts went on to reach the Scottish Cup final in 1995-96 but were beaten 5-1 by Rangers. Bruno remained a regular for the first half of the following season playing in the 4-3 defeat to Rangers in the League Cup final. However age caught up with him and his appearances became sporadic after Christmas.

Bruno's Hearts career stats were 49 games, one goal and two red cards. After a very short spell with Wigan Athletic, he returned to Italy for family reasons early in 1997-98. He is now an agent and television pundit but has continued to follow the fortunes of Hearts, returning to Edinburgh for charity events.

FACT 76
1996
ALLAN JOHNSTON'S
IBROX HAT-TRICK

On 20th January 1996 Hearts beat Rangers 3-0 at Ibrox. Allan Johnston scored a hat-trick, the first opposition player to do so there for 37 years.

Few gave Hearts a chance going into this game. They had not won at Ibrox since 1988 and Rangers were unbeaten in nineteen league games. However Johnston scored an early goal when he evaded his marker at the near post to head in John Colquhoun's cross.

After half an hour Hearts keeper Gilles Rousset saved brilliantly from Brian Laudrup to preserve the lead. It was Rangers' best chance of the game, as otherwise their attackers had been kept at bay by the outstanding Dave McPherson, playing his first game after a long injury lay off.

In the second half Hearts grew in belief and Johnston made it 2-0 when he coolly lobbed keeper Andy Goram from Neil Pointon's cross. With seven minutes remaining Pointon was the provider again, as Johnston side-stepped Goram to complete his hat-trick and a memorable win for Hearts.

Hearts players and fans celebrated ecstatically, especially Johnston who had become the first player to score a hat-trick at Ibrox since Sir Alex Ferguson, who did so as a player for St Johnstone in 1963.

FACT 77
1996 RED CARD FRENZY AT IBROX

The next time Hearts played at Ibrox following Allan Johnston's hat-trick was memorable for other reasons. The Jambos had four players sent off, the only time this has happened in the Scottish top-flight.

The first half was evenly matched but Hearts went a goal behind when Gordon Durie scored after forty minutes. A minute into the second half, Pasquale Bruno was sent off after receiving his second yellow card. Two minutes after Hearts were reduced to ten men, Paul Gascoigne scored a second for Rangers.

On the hour, David Weir received a straight red card after an off the ball clash with Durie. Three minutes later Neil Pointon kicked a goalpost in frustration after a corner rather than offside was given and he received a second yellow card.

The Jambos were reduced to seven men in the 67th minute when Paul Ritchie was sent off for dissent after disputing a refereeing decision. Rangers captain Richard Gough pleaded with referee Gerry Evans to use common sense but he refused to listen.

To their credit, Rangers didn't enforce their numerical superiority and simply kept possession, with Ally McCoist adding a third goal near the end. In an interview with the *Daily Record* in 2015 Jim Jefferies, Hearts manager on the day, said Bruno was the only deserved red card and it was the worst refereeing display he had ever seen.

FACT 78
1997
RECORD APPEARANCE HOLDER LEAVES

Gary MacKay, who has made more appearances for Hearts than any other player, left the club in 1997.

MacKay joined Hearts as a sixteen-year-old in 1980 and was an unused substitute for the first two league games of the 1980-81 season. He also came off the bench in two League Cup group games before establishing himself as a regular in the second half of the campaign.

For sixteen years MacKay was a dependable midfielder whose hard work allowed others to flourish. He endured relegation, celebrated promotion, had the agony of missing out on the Championship in 1986 and suffered cup final defeats

In 1987-88 MacKay was capped four times by Scotland and was awarded a testimonial by Hearts in 1991. When he left early in 1997-98 for Airdrie, he had played 640 competitive games for the Jambos, including 21 in Europe. In total he scored 64 goals, his most prolific season being 1986-87 when he got ten.

MacKay remained at Airdrie for two years and had a spell as manager there. Inducted into Hearts Hall of Fame in 2006, he now works as a football agent.

FACT 79
1998 SCOTTISH CUP TRIUMPH ENDS 36 YEAR WAIT

Hearts won the Scottish Cup in 1997-98, beating Rangers in the final to clinch their first trophy in 36 years.

Since winning the Scottish League Cup in 1962, Hearts had reached five cup finals but lost them all. The last two of those had been to Rangers, their opponents at Celtic Park (Hampden was being reconstructed) on 16th May.

The Jambos got off to a dream start when Colin Cameron converted a penalty in the second minute after Steve Fulton was felled. Towards the end of the first half, Hearts had a double let off when keeper Gilles Rousset saved Lorenzo Amoruso's long range effort, then Brian Laudrup hit the post.

Ten minutes into the second half Hearts were awarded a free kick for offside. Rousset pumped the ball up field and it was collected by Stephane Adam whose right foot shot was too powerful for the keeper.

With nine minutes to go Ally McCoist pulled a goal back for Rangers. The remaining minutes lasted like hours for Hearts fans and manager Jim Jefferies later said it was "the longest ten minutes of my life."

The final whistle marked the end of 36 years of frustration and the following day, 200,000 lined the streets as the victorious team toured Edinburgh in an open top bus.

FACT 80
2000
CAMERON INSPIRES CELTIC COMEBACK

When Hearts went 2-0 down at Celtic on 5th February 2000, midfielder Colin Cameron refused to accept another thrashing. He drove the team forward and the Jambos came back to win 3-2.

Hearts had lost 4-0 there earlier in the season and when they trailed 2-0 after 28 minutes of this game, must have feared a repeat of that score line or worse. Cameron had other ideas though and three minutes after Celtic's second goal he rushed forward from midfield to collect a pass and beat the keeper with a curling shot.

Cameron was an inspiration to his teammates, including recent recruits Fitzroy Simpson and Róbert Tomaschek. Others may have faltered in the atmosphere but they showed no signs of nerves alongside Cameron. After 55 minutes Cameron won the ball in his own half, surged forward and laid off for Simpson. He played a through ball to Gary Naysmith who fired it past the keeper into the roof of the net.

Celtic's confidence was shot and there was no question of Hearts settling for a draw. Cameron continued to drive the team forward and with eight minutes left Darren Jackson was fouled in the area. Cameron stepped up to convert the penalty, leading to euphoric celebrations amongst the travelling Jambos fans.

FACT 81

2000
YOUNGSTERS TRIUMPH
AT HAMPDEN

Hearts won the Scottish Youth Cup for the third time in 2000, beating favourites Rangers 5-3 in a thrilling final at Hampden Park.

This was the third time the young Jambos had reached the final and they had triumphed in the previous ones. However those finals had been at club grounds and this was their first involvement in one at the national stadium.

In front of 3,000 fans, Rangers played a fluid passing game that Hearts at times struggled to contend with. Despite this, the Jambos didn't resort to long ball tactics and were eventually rewarded for hard work, and clinical finishing.

Hearts took the lead three times, through two long range stunners from Neil Janczyk and a close-range finish by Alan McIlroy. On each of these occasions Rangers fought back to equalise but Hearts refused to be dejected and their determination was eventually rewarded.

Three minutes from time Darren Goldie made it 4-3 from a penalty kick and before Rangers could equalise for a fourth time, Ryan Davidson headed a fifth. During the game Hearts had just five efforts on target, scoring them all.

The triumph was the last time to date that Hearts won the Scottish Youth Cup. They have reached three more finals without success, the last being a 5-2 defeat to Motherwell in 2016.

FACT 82
2002
FOUR DERBY GOALS ON DEBUT

New signing Mark de Vries made an instant impact for Hearts on 11th August 2002, when he scored four times against Hibs at Tynecastle.

The six-foot four inch Dutch striker had come on as a substitute on the opening day of the season at Dundee, but a week later he was in from the start for the derby.

The Jambos were already 1-0 up when de Vries got his first goal five minutes before halftime. After receiving a pass from Jean-Louis Valois, he chested the ball down and hit an unstoppable shot past the keeper Tony Caig.

Hibs pulled a goal back six minutes into the second half but on 66 minutes de Vries scored again after Caig couldn't hold a shot by Valois.

Despite struggling with cramp, de Vries stayed on the pitch and in the final minute lifted the ball over the advancing Caig after Paul McMullan had crossed. Deep into injury time de Vries got his fourth when he rose to head home Gary Wales's cross.

De Vries had become the first Hearts player to score a hat-trick against Hibs in the Premier League. He was also the first to score four derby goals, emulating Joe Baker, who achieved the feat for Hibs in 1958.

FACT 83

2002
HEARTS STEAL THE SHOW AT EASTER ROAD

On 3rd November 2002 Hearts stunned Hibs at Easter Road, scoring twice in the last four minutes to beat their rivals 2-1.

Hibs had the better of the first half and felt they were unlucky to only have Mixu Paatelainen's 36th minute goal to show for their efforts. When the game restarted after half time Hibs remained on top and Hearts struggled to cope with Gary O'Connor's powerful runs.

Paatelainen almost scored a second for Hibs but his shot went just over the bar. At 1-0 Hearts always had a chance and four minutes from time Kevin McKenna headed an equaliser. Neither side were prepared to settle for the draw and Tam McManus struck a fierce free kick for Hibs that was well saved by Roddy McKenzie.

There were just seconds remaining when Hearts put together a fine passing move that ended with Stamp driving the ball home with a low left foot shot. The Jambos support went wild and Stamp was sent off when his excessive celebration was deemed worthy of a second yellow card.

Two months later Hearts again scored two late derby goals to deny Hibs victory in an even more dramatic finale.

FACT 84
2003 INJURY TIME DERBY COMEBACK

Two months after their late comeback to win at Easter Road, Hearts again stunned their rivals in one of the most thrilling Edinburgh derbies. On 2nd January 2003 the Jambos came from two goals down in injury time to draw 4-4 against Hibernian at Tynecastle.

Hearts fell behind after eleven minutes when Derek Townley seized a short backpass by Alan Maybury to score. Six minutes later Tam McManus headed Hibs into a 2-0 lead but Hearts received a lifeline after half an hour when Andy Kirk was felled in the area. Steven Pressley stepped forward and converted the penalty.

After 62 minutes Hearts were level when Mark de Vries rounded the keeper to score. However Craig James put Hibs back into the lead and they led 3-2 after ninety minutes.

Two minutes into stoppage time Hibs were awarded a penalty due to a handball by Pressley. Although Roddy McKenzie saved Mixu Paatelainen's spot kick he could do nothing to stop Grant Brebner scoring the rebound and Hibs looked to have sealed the victory.

In the fourth minute of injury time teenage substitute Graeme Weir scored what appeared to be a consolation, but just 42 seconds later Tynecastle erupted when he converted a de Vries cross to equalise.

FACT 85

2004
MURRAYFIELD

When Hearts qualified for the 2004-05 UEFA Cup, they had to play their home games at Murrayfield. This was because Tynecastle did not meet UEFA's pitch length requirements.

For the qualifying round against Braga, there were just 18,769 at the 63,000 capacity national rugby stadium. Rows of empty seats didn't put Hearts off though and they won 3-1, Patrick Kisnorbo scoring a crucial third goal in injury time. Two weeks later in Portugal, Hearts drew 2-2 to make it through to the group stage.

The competition format divided teams into groups of five, with the top three progressing. Teams played each other once, meaning Hearts had 'home' games at Murrayfield against German side Schalke and Ferencvárosi of Hungary.

After losing their opener 3-0 against Dutch giants Feyenoord in Rotterdam, Hearts faced Schalke at Murrayfield. In front of 27,272 fans, Hearts' task became harder when Kisnorbo was sent off early in the second half with the game goalless. Despite their best efforts, Hearts ended up losing 1-0.

A 2-1 victory over Basel in Switzerland gave Hearts hope of progressing to the knockout phase. They needed to beat Ferencvárosi at Murrayfield and hope Basel failed to beat Feyenoord at home. However their hopes were dashed when Ferencvárosi won 1-0 in a game watched by a crowd of 26,182.

FACT 86

2005
VLADIMIR ROMANOV

Hearts came under new ownership in 2005 when Vladimir Romanov took control of the club. It was a move that was welcome at the time, but eventually turned sour.

With the club in financial difficulties, the unthinkable notion of selling Tynecastle and moving into Murrayfield was mooted in 2004. Shareholder Romanov gradually increased his stake and a deal was agreed for him to take full control in January 2005.

The first full season under Romanov's control ended up with Hearts winning the Scottish Cup and finishing second in the league. However it was also one of managerial upheaval that saw George Burley sacked mid-season to be replaced by Graham Rix who later made way for Lithuanian Valdas Ivanauskas.

During 2006-07 it became clear that all was not well, as players began to speak out about Romanov's interference in the dressing room.

Romanov continued to change managers with alarming frequency. Ivanauskas cited stress when he left in 2007, then Anatoliy Korobochka and Stephen Frail didn't last long as results failed to improve. Csaba Laszlo and Jim Jefferies, back for a second spell in charge, were both dismissed despite third place finishes.

There was joy for Hearts fans when they won the Scottish Cup in 2012, but the club's debt was increasing. In 2013 the Lithuanian commercial bank Ukio Bankas collapsed, Romanov fled into exile and Hearts had no choice but to enter administration.

FACT 87
2006
PENALTIES DECIDE THE CUP FINAL

Hearts won the Scottish Cup in 2006, but needed penalties to overcome Gretna, the first side from the third tier to reach the final.

The Jambos were clear favourites having finished second in the Premier League. Although Gretna cruised to promotion they hadn't faced top flight opposition on their way to the final.

After having the better of the first half, Hearts took a deserved lead six minutes before the break when Rudi Skacel scored from close range. In the second half, Hearts were not as dominant but still looked to be in comfortable control of the game. However with fifteen minutes left they conceded a penalty and although Craig Gordon saved Ryan McGuffie's spot kick, he couldn't prevent the rebound going in.

In the first period of extra time Hearts hit the post, went close with a free kick and saw the keeper make a great save. With five minutes left Skacel was felled in the box but no penalty was given. Hearts were then struck a huge blow with penalties looming when their regular taker Paul Hartley was sent off for a second bookable foul.

When the shoot-out came it was the Jambos who held their nerve, converting all four necessary kicks to win 4-2, meaning the cup was going to Tynecastle for the seventh time.

FACT 88
2006 THE CHAMPIONS LEAGUE

Hearts second place finish in the Scottish Premier League in 2006 earned them a place in the Champions League qualifiers.

To make it into the lucrative group stages of Europe's premier competition, Hearts needed to negotiate two qualifying rounds. The first of these paired the Jambos with Bosnian side Široki Brijeg.

Hearts were again forced to play at Murrayfield as Tynecastle did not meet UEFA requirements. Hearts won the first leg 3-0, all the goals coming in the second half. They then drew 0-0 in Bosnia to seal their progress to the final qualifying round against AEK Athens.

In front of a crowd of over 32,000, a goal from Saulius Mikoliūnas gave Hearts the lead after an hour. However they were left with an uphill task for the second leg when AEK scored twice late on, the winner coming in stoppage time.

The second leg was played at the Olympic Stadium, which would be the venue for that season's final. Hearts fought bravely before three goals in the last eleven minutes ended their dreams of overturning the deficit.

Despite going out of the Champions League, Hearts had the compensation of dropping into the last qualifying round for the UEFA Cup. However they were again disappointed, losing 2-0 to Sparta Prague at Murrayfield before drawing 0-0 in the Czech Republic.

FACT 89
2007
BRITISH RECORD FEE
FOR A GOALKEEPER

When Craig Gordon was sold to Sunderland for £9 million in August 2007, it was the highest transfer fee paid for a goalkeeper by a British club.

A Scottish Youth Cup winner with Hearts in 2000, Gordon spent time on loan at Cowdenbeath before making his senior debut for the Jambos in October 2002. He became the first-choice keeper in 2003-04 and was named that season's SPL Young Player of the Year.

In 2005-06 Gordon was a key player as Hearts finished second in the league and won the Scottish Cup. The final against Gretna went to penalties and Gordon saved Derek Townsley's kick in the shootout which the Jambos won 4-2. He was named as the Football Writers Player of the Year and had established himself as the Scottish national side's regular keeper.

During 2006-07 Gordon became captain but there was continuing friction between some of the players and owner Vladimir Romanov. He played some pre-season games for Hearts but after being linked with moves to Arsenal and Aston Villa, it was Sunderland who agreed to pay the £9 million asking price.

Gordon became the youngest player to be inducted into Heart's Hall of Fame later that year. In June 2020 he re-joined Hearts after being released by Celtic where he had been since 2014.

FACT 90
2008
HEARTS YOUNGEST PLAYER

When Scott Robinson came on as a substitute for Hearts against Inverness Caldeonian Thistle on 26th April 2008, he became the club's youngest player in a competitive match.

Robinson joined Hearts as a fourteen-year-old in 2006 from Hutchison Vale Boys Club. He signed his first professional contract in April 2008, soon after his sixteenth birthday. The young striker had already represented Scotland at under 16 and 17 level.

In the game against Inverness at Tynecastle, Hearts were leading 1-0 when Robinson came on in injury time for goal scorer Gary Glen. At 16 years, 1 month and 14 days old, he was the youngest player ever to play for Hearts in a competitive game, as well as for any club in the Scottish Premier League.

This was Robinson's only appearance that season. For 2008-09 he returned to the reserves to develop his game further and was back in the first team picture the following season. His first goal was in a 1-1 draw against Rangers at Ibrox in January 2010. He remained at Hearts until 2015 when he signed for Kilmarnock.

FACT 91
2009
HEART OF MIDLOTHIAN LADIES

In 2009 Hearts launched their first women's team, who like their male counterparts were commonly known as Hearts Ladies rather than their full title.

Hearts took over Musselburgh Windsor Ladies FC, who had recently won promotion to the First Division of the Scottish Women's Football League, then the second tier. The club also announced their intention to have teams at various age groups to develop a pathway to the first team.

When the Scottish Women's Premier League was expanded in 2016 to create a second tier, Hearts Ladies were accepted. They finished second in their first season, two points behind Hamilton who were promoted.

In 2018 the name was changed to Hearts Women, with games to be played at The Oriam in Riccarton, venue for the club's academy and training base for the men's first team. This was to further integrate them into the wider club.

Significant investment was also promised and this paid off when they finished champions of SWPL2 in 2019, winning promotion to the top flight. However after just one game of 2020, the league was suspended due to the Coronavirus pandemic.

FACT 92

2012
THE GREATEST DAY
IN HEARTS HISTORY

On 19th May 2012 Hearts beat Hibs 5-1 in the Scottish Cup final, a day generally regarded amongst fans as the greatest day in the club's history.

It was the first all Edinburgh final since 1896 and many local politicians called for the game to be switched to Murrayfield which had a bigger capacity. However the SFA stated that no venue other than Hampden Park would be considered.

Hearts took control of the game from the start and deservedly went ahead through Darren Barr after fifteen minutes. Rudi Skacel doubled the lead after 27 minutes but Hibs pulled a goal before half time.

Three minutes after the restart Hearts restored their two-goal advantage. Danny Grainger converted a penalty which was awarded for a foul on Suso, for which Hibs defender Pa Kujabi received a second yellow card, reducing his side to ten men. Two minutes later Ryan McGowan headed the fourth goal and Skacel completed the rout fifteen minutes from time.

The following day thousands of fans turned out to see the players travel from Edinburgh City Chambers to Tynecastle on an open top bus, which had been decorated in maroon colours. Manger Paulo Sergio said it had been the greatest achievement of his career and that it was great to see the joy of supporters.

FACT 93
2013
ADMINISTRATION

Just one year on from the greatest day in Hearts history, the club was placed in administration with debts of £25 million.

Many of the side that won the Scottish Cup in 2012 left on the expiry of their contracts. Manager Paulo Sergio also moved on, citing the fact he was offered a deal on terms less than half of his previous one.

Throughout the season, salaries were paid late and the collapse of Vladmir Romanov's Lithuanian bank in May left the club in a dire situation. Failure to make payments to the Inland Revenue meant there was no other choice but to enter administration or face a winding up order.

Hearts were deducted fifteen points and barred from signing new players, meaning 2013-14 would be an uphill battle. However fans were just relieved to have a club to support as donations were sought for a fan backed takeover. In June 2014, Bidco, fronted by Ann Budge, took control to bring the Romanov era to an end.

Budge, a millionaire former IT specialist aimed at transferring control to the Foundation of Hearts in five years providing certain conditions were met. Although that has yet to happen, she rejected an offer from an American consortium in 2020 stating fan control was the preferred option.

FACT 94

2014
AN INEVITABLE RELEGATION

With a ban on new signings and fifteen-point deduction, Hearts were unsurprisingly relegated in 2013-14. However at the end of the season the ownership issue was resolved and the club could look to the future with confidence.

Hearts had a promising start, taking seven points from the first four games, including a 1-0 win over Hibs at Easter Road. However they lost seven out of their next eight games to remain adrift at the bottom. They didn't reach zero points until the 24th game, a 2-1 win at Ross County. This result left them nineteen points from safety and the thinness of the squad was emphasised by the fact only six substitutes were named.

On 30th March, Hearts faced the humiliating prospect of relegation being confirmed if they lost to Hibs at Tynecastle. Goals from Dale Carrick and Billy King staved that off, but despite beating Partick Thistle the following week, a win for St Mirren meant Hearts were down.

Hearts lost only one of their last five fixtures. One of these was a 2-1 win over Hibs at Easter Road that dragged their rivals into the mire. Hearts eventually finished bottom of the table while Hibs lost their play-off meaning for the first time ever, Edinburgh derbies would be taking place in the second tier.

FACT 95

2015
STRAIGHT BACK UP

Hearts cruised to promotion in 2014-15, finishing 21 points clear of second place Hibs at the top of the Championship.

With the club's ownership issue now resolved, Hearts were able to make new signings and there was also a change of manager, with Robbie Neilson replacing Gary Locke. It was an unusual Championship make up, with the Edinburgh clubs joined by Rangers. They were making their way back up the leagues after their own financial problems and expulsion from the Premiership.

Hearts made a statement in their opening game, with new signing Osman Sow hitting a stoppage time winner against Rangers at Ibrox. They won sixteen of their first eighteen games and at Hogmanay were fifteen points clear at the top.

Hearts were finally beaten in their 21st game when Falkirk won 3-2 at Tynecastle. They lost only three games all season, two of them after promotion was secured.

Confirmation of promotion came without kicking a ball. On 21st March Hearts won 3-0 at Falkirk then the following day Hibs 2-0 defeat at home to Rangers meant the Jambos couldn't be caught.

The following week, there was a carnival atmosphere at a sold out Tynecastle as Hearts celebrated in style, beating Queen of the South 2-0. By the season's end, their playing record was Won 29, Drawn 4, Lost 3.

FACT 96

2015 RECORD LEAGUE VICTORY

During Hearts memorable 2014-15 season they enjoyed their record league victory when Cowdenbeath were thrashed 10-0 at Tynecastle on 28th February 2015.

Amazingly it took the Jambos 26 minutes to score their first goal, Genero Zeefuik converting a penalty that was awarded for handball. A minute later he scored again then after 29 minutes Hearts were given another penalty for a foul on Billy King by Lewis Toshney, who was shown a straight red card. Zeefuik stepped forward again to complete his hat-trick.

Sam Nicholson and Jamie Walker both scored from outside the box to give Hearts a 5-0 half time lead. Twelve minutes after the restart Morgaro Gomis was fouled in the area and he took the penalty himself, cheekily chipping the ball down the middle.

The four goals that took the tally to double figures came in one thirteen-minute spell between the 61st and 74th minutes. Alim Ozturk scored with a great shot from 25 yards, Danny Wilson got one from close range after a corner and substitute Osman Sow hit the ninth and tenth.

Despite the huge victory, boss Robbie Neilson refused to get carried away and insisted his side had played better when coming from behind at Queen of the South the previous week.

FACT 97
2017
BACK TO TYNECASTLE PARK

The modernisation of Tynecastle was complete in 2017 with the construction of a new Main Stand. It also saw the official name revert back to Tynecastle Park after twenty years as Tynecastle Stadium.

Between 1994 and 1997 new stands were built on three sides of the ground. Tynecastle Park became Tynecastle Stadium but this was never popular with fans.

In 2004 there were fears that Tynecastle would be sold to a property development company, with Hearts renting Murrayfield from the Scottish Rugby Union. There was widespread opposition to this and the takeover by Vladimir Romanov ensured Hearts would be staying at Tynecastle, where the pitch was modified to meet UEFA regulations.

The club's financial circumstances meant that long running plans to replace the old Main Stand didn't take place until 2017. Construction of the 7,000 seat stand, which also included offices and a nursery, took longer than anticipated. Although League Cup games could be played at Tynecastle with a reduced capacity, four home games in the SPL were played at Murrayfield.

On 19th November 2017 Hearts played their first league game of the season at Tynecastle, drawing 1-1 with Partick Thistle. The stadium was also officially renamed Tynecastle Park.

FACT 98

2017
BRINGING CELTIC'S RECORD TO AN END

On 17th December 2017 Hearts thrashed Celtic 4-0 at Tynecastle, ending their record of 69 domestic games unbeaten.

Celtic's unbeaten record in domestic competition stretched back to May 2016 but Hearts were not intimidated and dominated the early stages of the game. They refused to let Celtic settle and pressed at every opportunity.

After 26 minutes Hearts were rewarded when Don Cowie seized on a slip and passed the ball to teenager Harry Cochrane who made no mistake. Kyle Lafferty made it 2-0 nine minutes later with a shot that went in off the post and the noise from the home fans at the half time whistle was deafening.

Early in the second half Manuel Milinkovic scored an easy third for Hearts, rounding the keeper to slot home after Celtic defender Jozo Šimunović misjudged the bounce of the ball. Despite trying everything to get back in the game and Celtic manager Brendan Rodgers sending on extra attackers, Hearts defence was rock solid.

With fifteen minutes left, any worries of a comeback were forgotten when Milinkovic scored from the penalty spot after Ross Callachan was fouled. The final 4-0 score line didn't flatter Hearts, who had achieved their biggest victory over Celtic since 1895.

FACT 99
2019
HEARTS OLDEST OUTFIELD PLAYER

When Hearts lost 2-1 at Celtic on the last day of the 2018-19 season, Aaron Hughes came on as a second half substitute to become the oldest outfield player in their history.

Hughes was 37 years old when he joined Hearts in the January 2017 transfer window. The experienced defender had played 455 top-flight games in England and been capped over 100 times by Northern Ireland.

Initially signed until the end of the season, Hughes impressed enough to be given a one-year extension. He made 23 league appearances in 2017-18 but despite being given another deal, was used sparingly the following season and started just three games.

Hughes came on against Celtic in the 67th minute for his fourth substitute appearance of the season. He was 39 years, 6 months and 10 days old. The previous record holder was Sandy Jardine, who was 38 years 8 months and 27 days old when he played against Dunfermline in 1987.

The defender just missed out on being the oldest player in any position. He was just one day younger than goalkeeper Henry Smith was when he played a League Cup tie at Dundee in 1995. Hughes left the club at the end of May 2019 and the following month announced his retirement from football.

FACT 100
2020 AN UNJUST RELEGATION

Hearts were relegated in the cruellest of circumstances in 2019-20 when the Scottish Premier League was ended early due to the Coronavirus pandemic.

When football was suspended in the middle of March, the Jambos were bottom of the table and four points adrift of Hamilton Academical. There eight games remaining, one of which would have been against the Accies.

On 18th May, league bosses opted to end the season early and decide positions on a points per game basis, condemning Hearts to the Championship.

A furious Ann Budge was unable to gain enough support for league reconstruction that would have seen a fourteen team top-flight for 2020-21. There was then a legal challenge to overturn the decision, but a three strong panel at the Court of Session ruled the relegation was lawful.

Following the announcement, the club released a joint statement with Partick Thistle, relegated to League One in similar circumstances. It said "All we can only say is how disappointed and surprised we are at the outcome. We don't regret taking this action as it was the right thing for us to do. There were better ways to deal with ending the season, fairer ways other than putting the burden of a pandemic on to three clubs."

The 100 Facts Series

Arsenal, *Steve Horton*	978-1-908724-09-0
Aston Villa, *Steve Horton*	978-1-908724-98-4
Celtic, *Steve Horton*	978-1-908724-10-6
Chelsea, *Kristian Downer*	978-1-908724-11-3
Everton, *Bob Sharp*	978-1-908724-12-0
Hearts, *Steve Horton*	978-1-912782-48-2
Leeds, *Steve Horton*	978-1-908724-94-6
Leicester City, *Steve Horton*	978-1-912782-47-5
Liverpool, *Steve Horton*	978-1-908724-13-7
Manchester City, *Steve Horton*	978-1-908724-14-4
Manchester United, *Iain McCartney*	978-1-908724-15-1
Newcastle United, *Steve Horton*	978-1-908724-16-8
Norwich City, *Steve Horton*	978-1-908724-99-1
Nottingham Forest, *Steve Horton*	978-1-912782-46-8
Rangers, *David Clayton*	978-1-908724-17-5
Sheffield United, *Steve Horton*	978-1-912782-45-1
Tottenham Hotspur, *Steve Horton*	978-1-908724-18-2
West Ham, *Steve Horton*	978-1-908724-80-9

Player Autographs

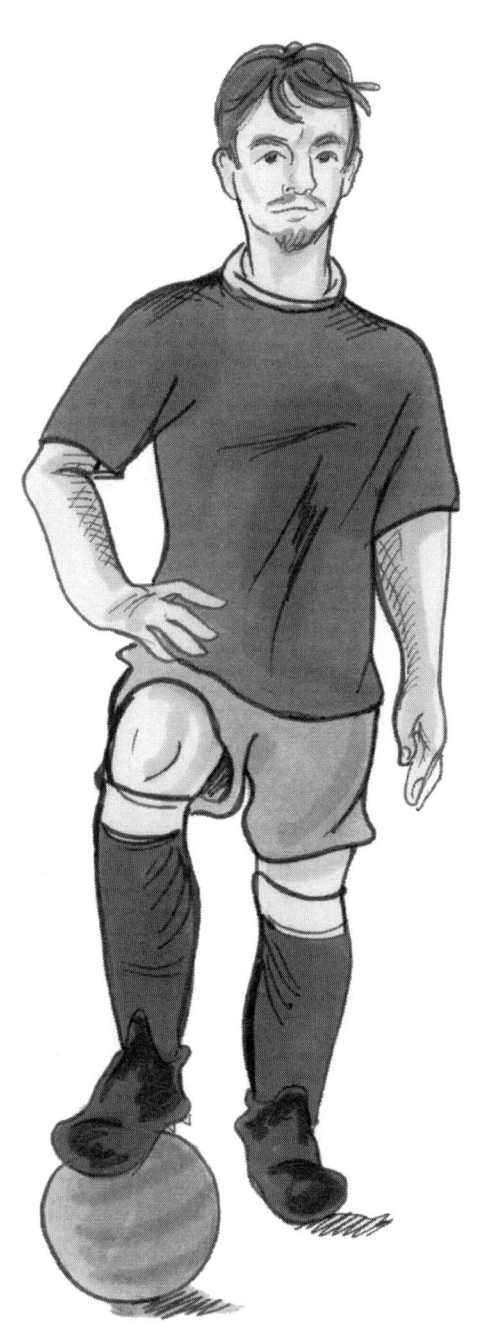

Player Autographs

Player Autographs

Player Autographs

Player Autographs

Player Autographs

Player Autographs